MW01132316

PETER

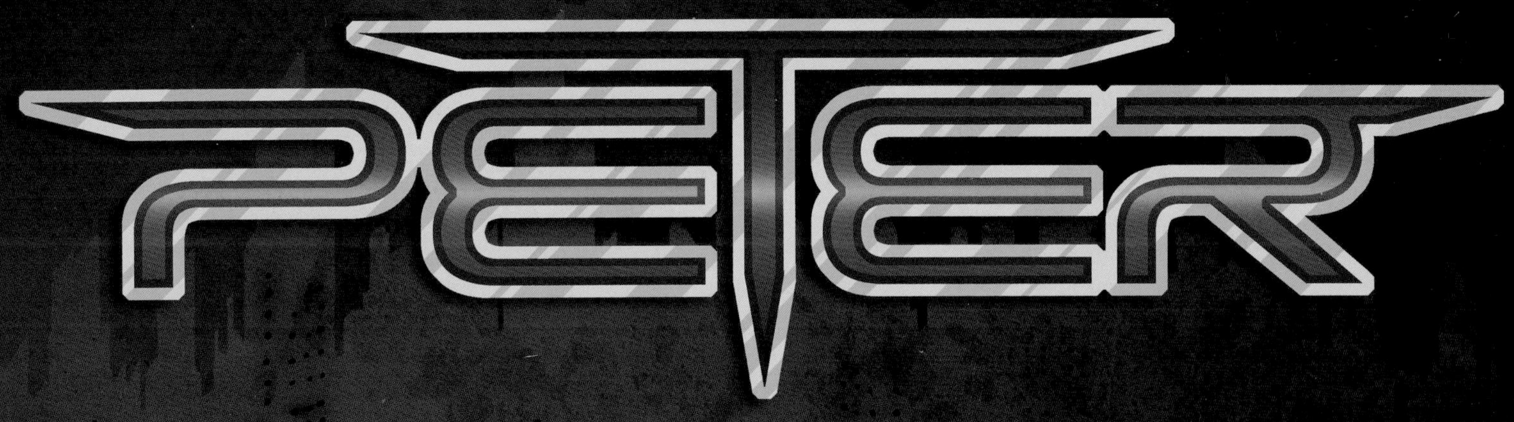

THE APOSTLE

GRAPHIC STORY BIBLE

BEN AVERY MARK HARMON

MARIO DEMATTEO ISMAEL CASTRO

CREDITS:

MARIO DEMATTEO

CREATOR / CO-WRITER / ART DIRECTOR

BEN AVERY

WRITER

MARK HARMON

ILLUSTRATOR / INKER

ISMAEL CASTRO

COLORIST / ASSISTANT INKER / LETTERER

MARCOS MUJICA

BIBLE CONSULTANT

BroadStreet Publishing Group, LLC
8646 Eagle Creek Circle, Suite 210
Savage, MN 55378

Peter the Apostle: Graphic Story Bible

9781424552757

Printed in China

I absolutely love the Graphic Story Bible series and so does my daughter! We have both been profoundly impacted by these resources: the messages, design and beautiful artwork have made these stories come alive for us. We have loved strengthening our faith through these graphic novels. They are well written, beautifully illustrated, biblical and encouraging!

-**Erin Weidemann**, founder of Truth Becomes Her and author of the best-selling Bible Belles series

The Graphic Story Bible series captures the drama and truth of the Bible in a visually stunning way. This series will surely attract countless children to the Good News of Jesus Christ.

-**Dr. Brian Simmons**, The Passion Translation Project

The Graphic Story Bible series is a brilliant rendition of action-packed drama and real life Bible lessons, which are beautifully and accurately illustrated. Children and adults alike will deeply appreciate the creative talents of the Graphic Story Bible team as the New Testament comes to life.

-**Brenda Crouch**, author, speaker, TV host

What a gift to have such an engaging and artistic book to share the Gospel message with my children.

-**Abby Barrantes**, youth director, teacher, mom

Peter the Apostle: Graphic Story Bible is so cool. I love all the colorful characters and epic lands. My favorite scene is when Jesus saves the demon-possessed man from the scary demon named Legion.

-**Samuel**. 9 years old

I loved that the story didn't end with Christ, but then went on to share Peter's journey as an apostle. It mirrors the idea that our journey doesn't end with Christ, but merely begins with Christ as we seek to follow him in our own lives.

-**Isaiah**, 14 years old

This book is incredible! It was very engaging and helpful for me to share the good news with my friends!

-**Mari**, 12 years old

THANKS FOR CHECKING OUT PETER THE APOSTLE.

IN YOUR HANDS IS THE SECOND INSTALLMENT OF OUR FUTURISTIC GRAPHIC STORY BIBLE COME TO LIFE. WE PRAY YOU'LL FALL IN LOVE WITH THE POWERFUL STORIES, THE CHARACTERS, AND THE GRAPHIC NOVEL ART, ALL WHILE LEARNING ABOUT GREAT BIBLE HEROES YOU CAN LOOK UP TO IN YOUR OWN LIFE.

OUR INTENTION HAS ALWAYS BEEN ONE OF MINISTRY AND EDUCATION. WE'RE USING A FUTURISTIC GRAPHIC NOVEL LANGUAGE TO ILLUMINATE THE STORY OF PETER THE APOSTLE AND ULTIMATELY, THE MESSAGE OF JESUS CHRIST. IN NO WAY ARE WE TRYING TO REPLACE THE BIBLE OR ENHANCE IT. THE WORD OF GOD IS ALREADY AWESOME AND PERFECT! FOR THIS REASON, WE STRIVE FOR OUR ADAPTION OF THE LIFE OF PETER AND ALL FUTURE ADAPTATIONS TO BE ACCURATE PORTRAYALS OF THE BIBLICAL ACCOUNT. WE'VE INCLUDED SCRIPTURAL REFERENCES AT THE BOTTOM OF PAGES THROUGHOUT THE BOOK TO INSPIRE READERS TO GO CHECK OUT WHERE ALL THIS AWESOMENESS ACTUALLY COMES FROM: THE BIBLE! WE HOPE YOU ENJOY THIS GRAPHIC NOVEL!

PROLOGUE

THE HOLY LAND WAS IN TURMOIL. FOR CENTURIES, THE JEWISH PEOPLE WERE CONTROLLED BY THE EVIL ROMAN EMPIRE. THOSE BRAVE ENOUGH TO STAND UP TO THE EMPIRE WERE QUICKLY DESTROYED. THE JEWISH PROPHETS FORETOLD THE COMING OF AN ALL-POWERFUL KING OF KINGS, A HOLY MESSIAH, WHO WOULD FREE THEM FROM THE CLUTCHES OF THE ROMAN EMPIRE AND RESTORE PEACE AND PROSPERITY TO GOD'S CHOSEN PEOPLE. WHISPERS OF REVOLUTION WERE HEAVY IN THE AIR. FEW EXPECTED THE TRUE KING AND HOLY MESSIAH WOULD BRING A REVOLUTION NOT OF FORCE AND VIOLENCE, BUT OF REPENTANCE, FORGIVENESS, AND LOVE. THIS IS THE STORY OF AN ORDINARY MAN, WHOSE ENTIRE LIFE WAS FLIPPED UPSIDE DOWN WHEN HE WAS CALLED TO FOLLOW THE TRUE KING OF KINGS.

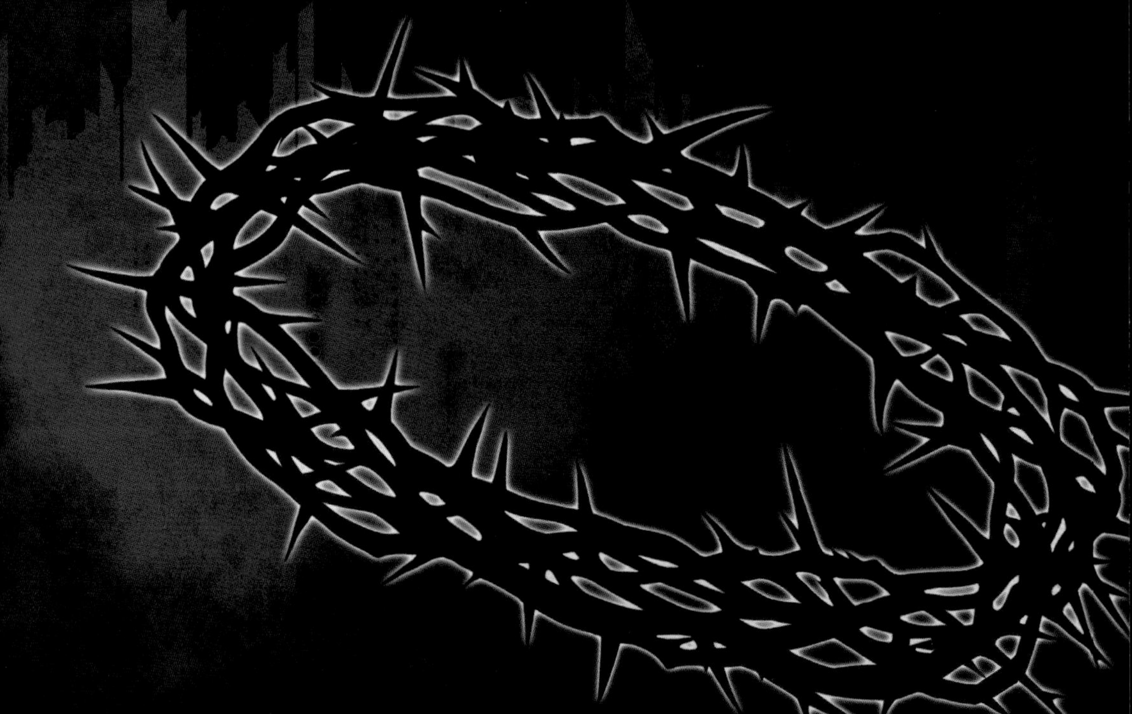

CHAPTER ONE:
THE CALLING

YOU ARE A CHOSEN PEOPLE. YOU ARE ROYAL PRIESTS, A HOLY NATION, GOD'S VERY OWN POSSESSION. AS A RESULT, YOU CAN SHOW OTHERS THE GOODNESS OF GOD, FOR HE CALLED YOU OUT OF THE DARKNESS INTO HIS WONDERFUL LIGHT. "ONCE YOU HAD NO IDENTITY AS A PEOPLE; NOW YOU ARE GOD'S PEOPLE. ONCE YOU RECEIVED NO MERCY; NOW YOU HAVE RECEIVED GOD'S MERCY.

–1 PETER 2:9–10

JERUSALEM, 43 A.D.
A PALACE BUILT BY HEROD THE GREAT.
NOW, A PRISON FOR THE WORST ENEMIES OF KING HEROD AGRIPPA.
CRIMINALS, TRAITORS, MURDERERS, THIEVES.
AND ME.
PETER.

WHATCHA LOOKIN' AT OUT THERE, EH?
YOU THINK YOU GONNA MAKE A PRISON BREAK?
THERE BE SIXTEEN OF US! BEST OF THE BEST!
YOU AIN'T GOIN' NOWHERE.
I DO NOT EXPECT TO ESCAPE.
I HAVE HOPE BEYOND THIS LIFE--
OH, HO! YOU GONNA BE RESURRECTED?
BOY-O, I HOPE WE GUARD YOU WHEN YOU'RE DEAD!
WE'LL GUARD YOUR DEAD BODY WAY BETTER THAN THEM LOSERS WHO GUARDED YOUR JESUS...
...WHEN YOU STINKIN' CHRISTIANS CAME AND STOLE HIM!
WE DID NOT STEAL HIS BODY!!!
HEY, HEY, HEY!!!

NONE OF THAT, NOW!
WE'RE IN CONTROL. DON'T YOU FORGET.
YOU CAN ONLY HARM MY BODY.
YEAH, AND SOON WE WILL!
THE FESTIVAL OF UNLEAVENED BREAD BRINGS JEWS FROM ALL OVER.
THEY'RE GONNA LOVE WATCHING YOU DIE TOMORROW.
HAHAHAH!
GET SOME REST NOW!
BEIN' EXECUTED IS HARD WORK!
BWHAAAA-HAAAA!

SHUT IT!
"BEING LEAD WHERE I DON'T WANT TO GO."
IS THIS WHAT JESUS MEANT?
IS THIS THE END?
OH, LORD.
IF THIS REALLY IS THE END...
...I SHOULD SPEND IT IN...
...PRAYER.
PETER?
PETER!

WAKE UP, PETER!
PETER, QUICKLY!
GET UP!
HUH? WHA--?
GET UP!
QUICKLY NOW!
!
AM I DREAMING?
NO. YOU MUST COME WITH ME.
WHAT'S GOING ON HERE?
NOT A DREAM, EH?
RIIIIIGHT.

ACTS 12:7-8

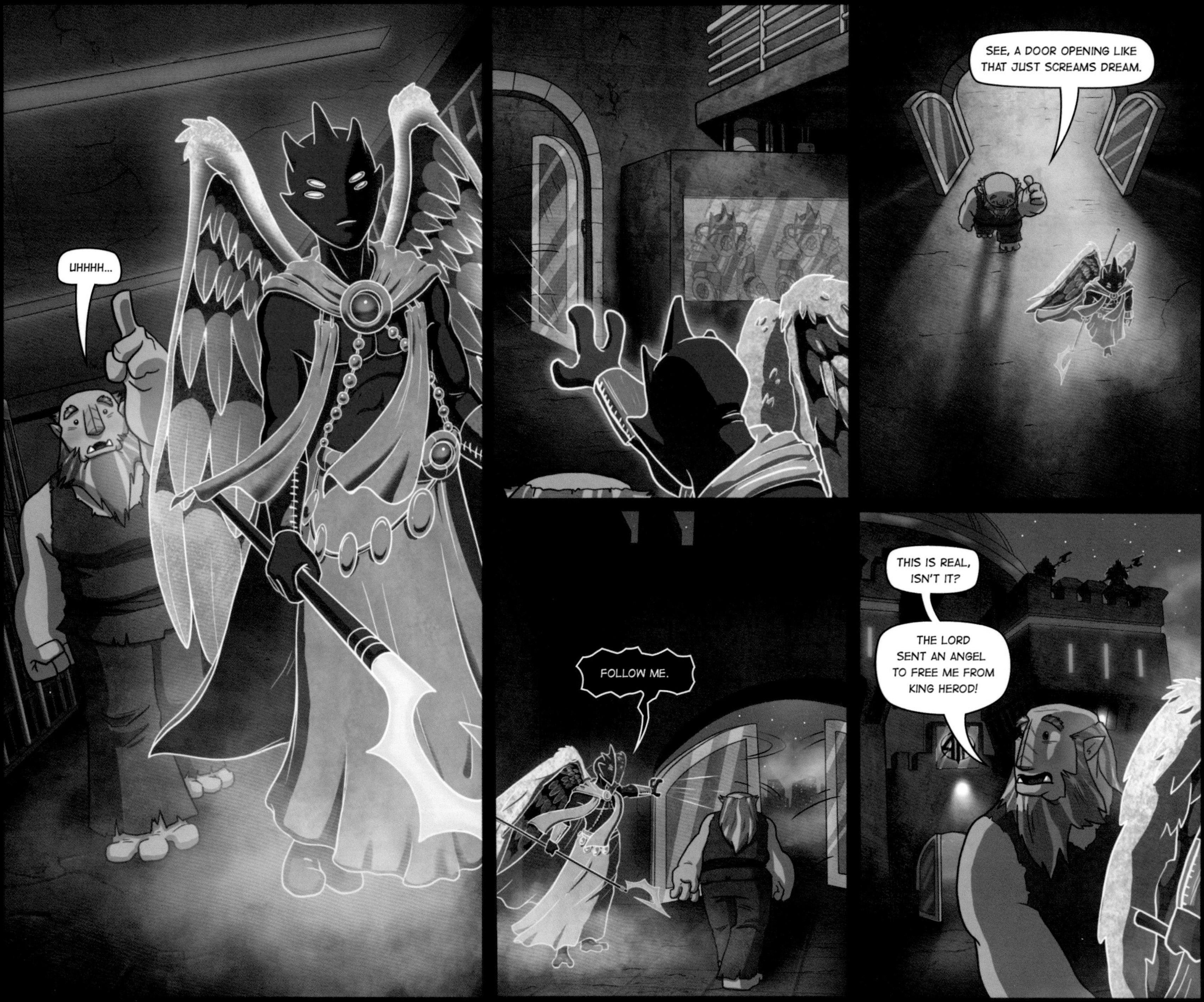

UHHHH...

FOLLOW ME.

YOU WERE SENT TO SAVE ME!
NOW WHAT?
WHAT'S GOING ON OVER THERE?

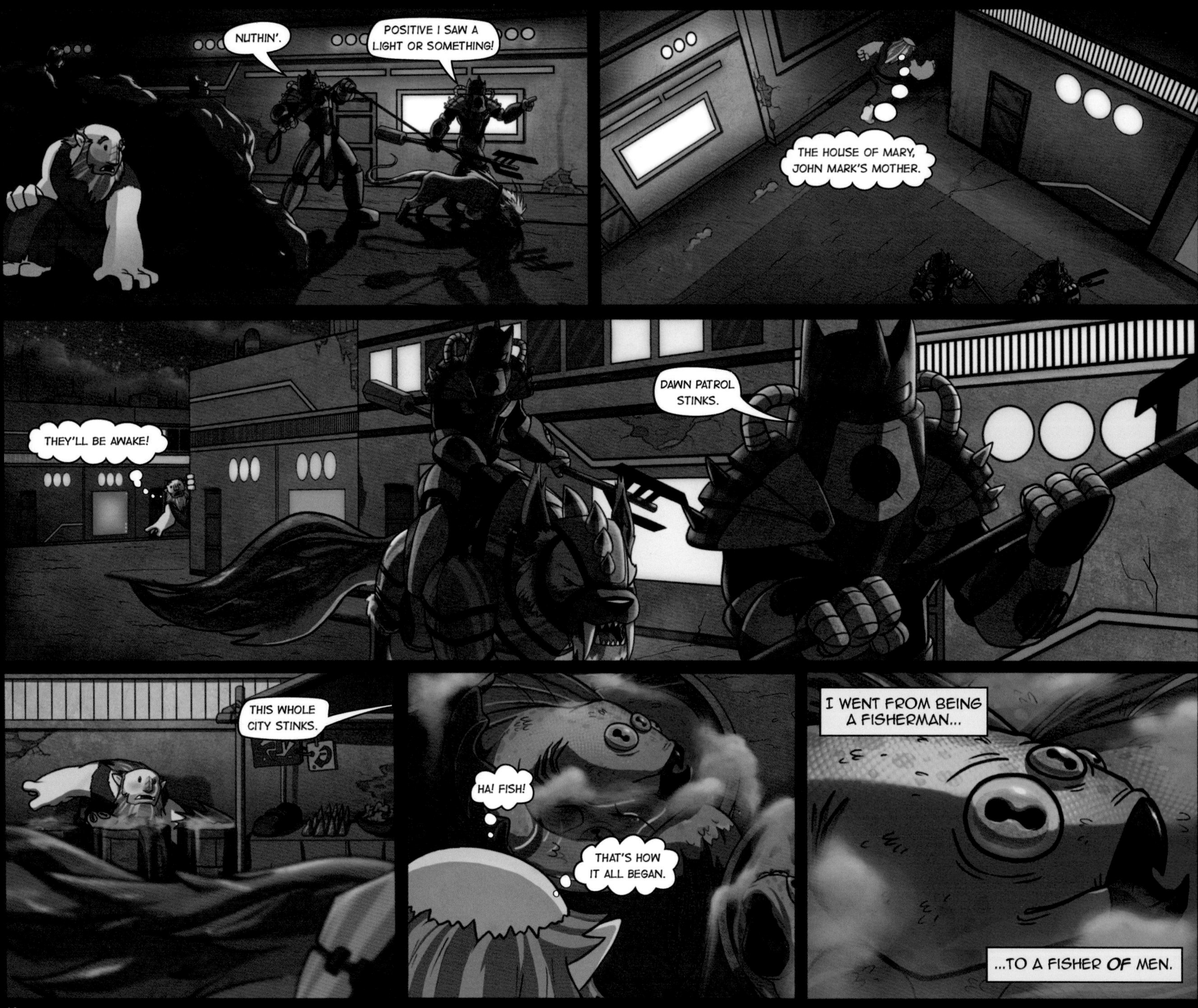

NUTHIN'.
POSITIVE I SAW A LIGHT OR SOMETHING!
THE HOUSE OF MARY, JOHN MARK'S MOTHER.
THEY'LL BE AWAKE!
DAWN PATROL STINKS.

IT WAS AROUND THE YEAR 29 A.D.
WHEN EVERYTHING IN MY LIFE CHANGED.

PULL, MEN!
PULL!!!

C'MON, BOYS!
A COUPLE GOT AWAY!
DOIN' ME BEST, SIMON!

WHAT DO YOU SAY, SIMON?
ANOTHER RUN WITH THE NETS?
HMMM...

NOT SURE IT'D BE WORTH IT, ANDREW.
SUN'S COMING UP.
YEAH, YOU'RE RIGHT.

CALL IT A DAY, BOYS.
ALRIGHT!
GET THIS NET STRAIGHTENED AND FOLDED!
AND THEN GET READY ON THE OARS!

I GOT A LOT MORE YESTERDAY FOR A SMALLER CATCH!
YEAH. YEAH. ROME RAISED TAXES AGAIN.
HIGHER TAXES MEANS LESS MONEY.
TAKE YOUR PROBLEMS TO THE EMPEROR OF ROME!

RAISED TAXES, HE SAYS!
I BET HIS TAX COLLECTOR IS CHEATING HIM.
SAME WAY OURS CHEATS US!

I'D RATHER PAY UNFAIR TAXES THAN GET ARRESTED
SOMETIMES, I WONDER IF THE REBELS ARE RIGHT.
ARE YOU GOING HOME, ANDREW?

NOT YET. I'M GOING TO THE RIVER TO SEE JOHN THE BAPTIZER
AGAIN?
YES! PEOPLE SAY HE HAS THE "SPIRIT OF ELIJAH."

HE SAYS HE'S PREPARING PEOPLE FOR THE COMING OF THE MESSIAH!

THE MESSIAH?
IN OUR LIFETIME?

WHAT IF JOHN IS RIGHT?
THE WAY HE SPEAKS, SIMON.

IT'S LIKE HE'S A PROPHET.

COME WITH ME!
NAH, NOT TODAY. TOO TIRED.

MAYBE ANOTHER TIME.

WELCOME HOME, MY LOVE.
IT WAS A GOOD CATCH TODAY.
A GOOD CATCH.
HOW'S YOUR MOTHER?

NOT GOOD.
THE FEVER WON'T COME DOWN NO MATTER WHAT I DO.
I'M AFRAID SHE WON'T...

I MEAN, THERE'S NOT MUCH TIME...

I DON'T KNOW WHAT ELSE TO DO FOR HER.
SHE'S IN GOOD HANDS.
YOURS AND GOD'S.

SIMON!
SIMON, YOU'VE GOT TO HEAR THIS!!!

YOU'RE NOT GOING TO BELIEVE IT!
HELLO, ANDREW.
SURE, COME RIGHT IN.

SORRY...
I'M A BIT...EXCITED!
WHAT'S GOING ON?

BROTHER, THE MESSIAH!
HE'S...HE'S... REAL!

I'VE MET HIM!

COME WITH ME!
HE'S REAL! THE BAPTIZER WAS RIGHT!
MY LOVE---?
GO! GO!

JOHN 1:40-41

MATTHEW 3:13–17; MARK 1:9–11; LUKE 3:21–22; JOHN 1:35–39

YES. YOU ARE.
BUT YOU WILL BE CALLED PETER.
THE ROCK.

WAIT, IS HE SERIOUS?
LISTEN.

PEOPLE SAY, "LOVE YOUR NEIGHBOR AND HATE YOUR ENEMY."

BUT I SAY, "LOVE YOUR ENEMY."

PRAY FOR THEM AND DO GOOD TO THEM--
WHAT DO YOU THINK...PETER?

HE TEACHES THINGS I WISH OTHER RABBIS WOULD SAY.
BUT GREAT TEACHING DOESN'T MAKE HIM THE MESSIAH.

JOHN 1:42

I FOLLOWED NEWS OF JESUS AFTER THAT.
NOTHING!
LITERALLY NOTHING!!!
LET'S KEEP TRYING.

PEOPLE CAME FROM ALL OVER TO HEAR HIS TEACHINGS AND HIS CONFRONTATIONS WITH THE AUTHORITIES.
WHY ARE YOU DOING THIS TO US, LORD?
WHOA, SIMON, CALM DOWN.

BUT I STILL DID NOT FOLLOW HIM.
NEVER HAD A NIGHT THIS BAD...
EVER!!!
LOOK, OVER THERE!
IT'S HIM!

HELLO, PETER!
COULD I USE YOUR BOAT?
I NEED A PLACE WHERE EVERYONE CAN HEAR ME BUT IS NOT TOO CROWDED...

HE TAUGHT THE PEOPLE THAT DAY.
FROM *MY* BOAT!
IT WAS NICE TO LISTEN.
BUT THEN SOMETHING UNBELIEVABLE HAPPENED.

WHY DON'T YOU GO BACK OUT?
PUT YOUR NETS BACK OUT IN THE DEEP?
UH, RABBI, YOU'RE WISE ABOUT SPIRITUAL THINGS AND STUFF.
BUT I'VE BEEN FISHING ALL MY LIFE.

THE FISH AREN'T OUT THIS TIME OF DAY.
AND WE WERE OUT ALL NIGHT AND LITERALLY CAUGHT NOTHING.
IT WAS LIKE GOD WAS HOLDING THEM BACK FROM OUR NETS!

BUT...
...BECAUSE IT'S YOU JESUS...
...WE'LL DO IT.

LUKE 5:4–5

OUT ALL NIGHT WITH NOTHING TO SHOW FOR IT.
HERE HALF THE DAY, LETTING HIM USE OUR BOAT AS A PODIUM.
AND NOW BACK OUT ON A FOOL'S ERRAND--

WHA--???
AHHHK!!!

WE'RE GOING DOWN, SIMON!
WELL, WE'RE CERTAINLY NOT GOING FORWARD!
WHAT HAPPENED?

THE NETS CAUGHT SOMETHING!
FISH!!!
THEY'RE FULL OF FISH!

I CAN SIGNAL JAMES AND JOHN!
THEY CAN HELP!
IT'S NO USE!
WE'RE GONNA NEED A BIGGER BOAT!

LUKE 5:6

WE'RE EITHER GOING TO LOSE THE SHIP...
...OR LOSE THE CATCH!

WE'RE STABLE NOW! LET'S JUST TAKE IT IN LIKE THIS!
WE'LL FOLLOW YOUR LEAD AND MATCH YOUR SPEED!

THIS SHOULDN'T...
IT COULDN'T...

WHAT SEEMS TO BE THE TROUBLE, SIMON?
IT'S FISH!
IT'S ALL FISH!!!

HOW...
...IS IT TRUE?

LUKE 5:7

MATTHEW 4:18–20; MARK 1:16–18; LUKE 5:8–11

CHAPTER TWO: FOLLOW HIM

FOR WE WERE NOT MAKING UP CLEVER STORIES WHEN WE TOLD YOU ABOUT THE POWERFUL COMING OF OUR LORD JESUS CHRIST. WE SAW HIS MAJESTIC SPLENDOR WITH OUR OWN EYES.

–2 PETER 1:16

"A FISHER OF MEN."
I HAD NO IDEA WHAT THAT TRULY MEANT.
LOOKING BACK, THERE ARE MANY CHOICES I REGRET.
WHICH WAY...?
BUT THE CHOICE TO FOLLOW JESUS THAT DAY?
I'LL NEVER REGRET THAT.
EVEN CONSIDERING ALL THAT HAPPENED AFTERWARD.

AW, C'MON!
BZZZZZZT
HELLO? HI?
WHO'S OUT THERE?
IT'S ME RHODA. IT'S PETER!
SORRY, PETER'S NOT HERE!
HE'S IN JAIL!
NO! I'M NOT!
IT'S ME! PLEASE LET ME IN RHODA!
AMAZING!
YOU SOUND JUST LIKE HIM!
THAT'S BECAUSE I AM HIM!
PETER? IT'S REALLY YOU!
I MUST TELL THE MASTER!
WAIT! NO!

RHODA!
NOW WOULD BE A GOOD TIME TO LET ME IN.
TWO MINUTES AGO WOULD BE BETTER, BUT NOW IS JUST FINE, TOO.
RHODA?
PLEASE?
HEY, PETER, THEY DON'T BELIEVE ME.
WHAT???
WELL, THEY THINK YOU'RE YOUR ANGEL.
THEY DON'T BELIEVE YOU'RE YOU.
JUST OPEN THE DOOR, RHODA!
LET ME IN!
RHODA, YOU KNOW IT'S ME!
BZZZZZT!
PLEASE LET ME--

ACTS 12:14–15

IT IS YOU!
SHUT THE DOOR! SHUT THE DOOR!

SO GOOD TO SEE YOU, BUT HOW--
WE WERE PRAYING FOR YOU--
TOLD YOU, BUT YOU DIDN'T BELIEVE--
STOP, EVERYONE!

I'LL TELL YOU EVERYTHING!
BUT FIRST, I'M STARVING!
THAT PRISON FOOD WAS AWFUL!

...AND THE ANGEL DISAPPEARED INTO THE SKY AND THEN I CAME STRAIGHT HERE.
YOU KNOW WHAT'S ASTOUNDING AND AMAZING?
ASTOUNDING! AMAZING!

THAT FISH STEW!
ALMOST AS GOOD AS MY WIFE'S!
OH, YOU...

YOU SHOULDN'T BE HERE MUCH LONGER!
THEY'RE GONNA BE LOOKING FOR YOU, Y'KNOW!
I KNOW.
YOU JUST WAIT THERE!
I'LL MAKE ARRANGEMENTS TO GET YOU OUTTA HERE!
SO DO THINGS LIKE HAVING AN ANGEL BREAK YOU OUT OF PRISON EVEN SURPRISE YOU ANYMORE?
I MEAN, CONSIDERING YOU SAW SO MANY THINGS WHEN YOU WERE FOLLOWING JESUS!
THE POWER OF GOD ALWAYS AMAZES ME!
AND I DON'T KNOW IF WE EVER GOT USED TO THE MIRACLES JESUS DID.
I WOULD LOVE TO HAVE SEEN AN ACTUAL MIRACLE FROM JESUS!
IT WAS... SOMETHING ELSE.
BUT THE MIRACLES WERE JUST PART OF IT.
IT'S HARD TO EXPLAIN.
IN THOSE EARLY DAYS, WHEN I STARTED FOLLOWING HIM, NOBODY KNEW WHAT TO EXPECT.

MARK 1:21-24; LUKE 4:31-34

JESUSSSSSS OF NAZZZZZARETH!!!
WHY HAVE YOU COME?
HAVE YOU COME TO DESSSSTRRRROY US?
YOU'RE THE HOLY ONE OF GOD--
I KNOW YOU!
STOP SPEAKING!!!
EVIL SPIRIT!!!
COME OUT OF THAT MAN!!!
MARK 1:24-25; LUKE 4:34-35

MARK 1:25–30; LUKE 4:35–38

MATTHEW 8:14–15; MARK 1:31; LUKE 4:39

MATTHEW 8:15; MARK 1:31; LUKE 4:39

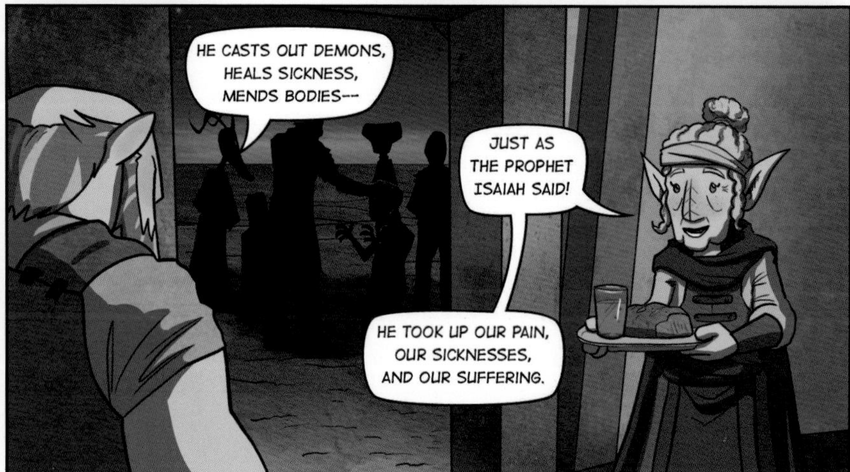

ISAIAH 53:4; MATTHEW 8:16; MARK 1:32-34; LUKE 4:40-41

MATTHEW 8:17; MARK 1:35-39; LUKE 4:42-43

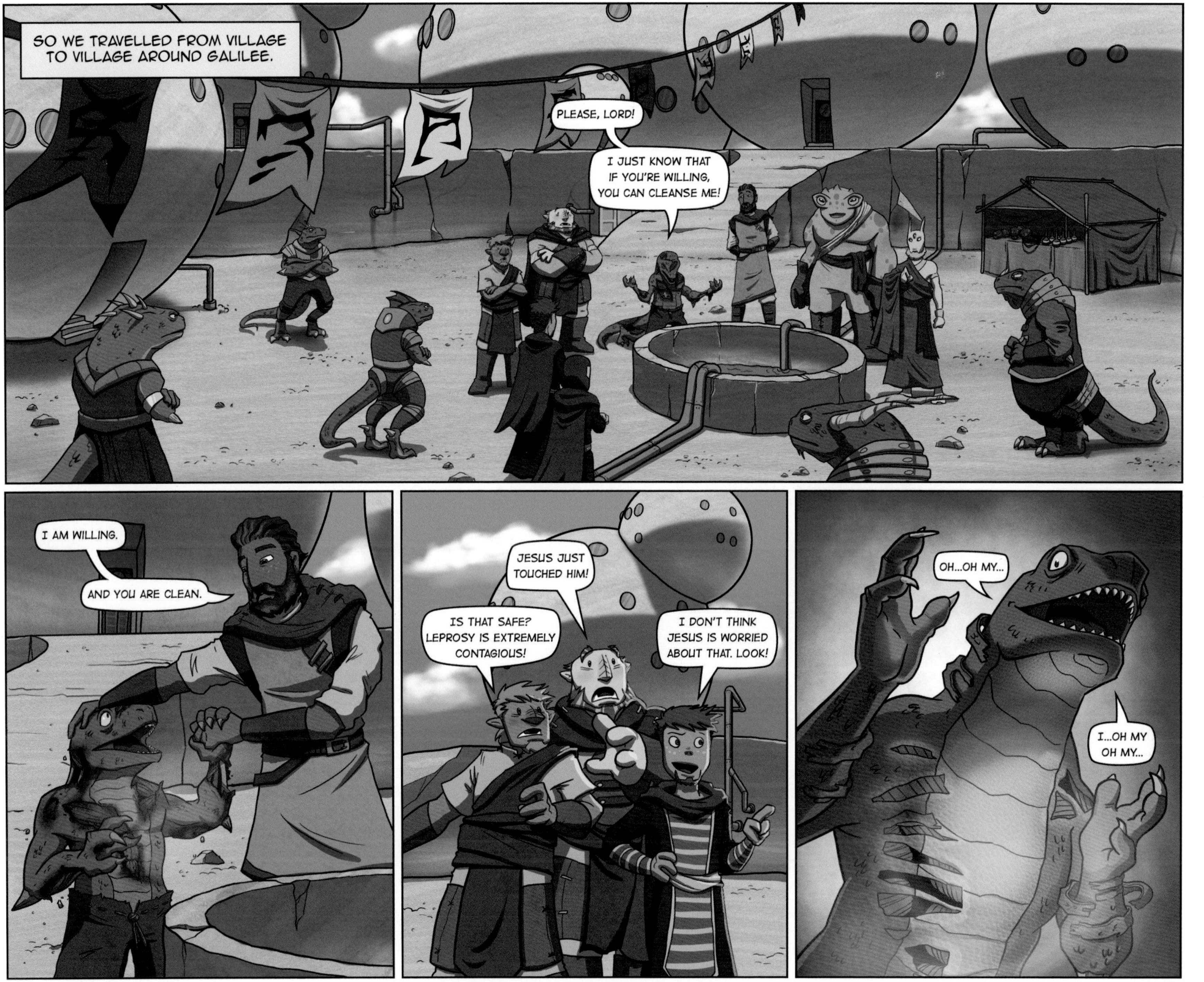

SO WE TRAVELLED FROM VILLAGE TO VILLAGE AROUND GALILEE.

PLEASE, LORD!

I JUST KNOW THAT IF YOU'RE WILLING, YOU CAN CLEANSE ME!

MATTHEW 8:2–3; MARK 1:40–42; LUKE 5:12–13

MATTHEW 8:4; MARK 1:43–45; LUKE 5:14–15

MATTHEW 9:2; MARK 2:1–3; LUKE 5:17–18

...TO BE SEEN BY MEN.

CAREFUL, LADS! DON'T WANT IT TO FALL!

MARK 2:4; LUKE 5:19

MATTHEW 9:2–6; MARK 2:5–10; LUKE 5:20–24

MATTHEW 9:6–8; MARK 2:11–12; LUKE 5:24–26

MATTHEW 9:9; MARK 2:13–14; LUKE 5:27–28, 6:27–28

MATTHEW 9:10–11; MARK 2:15–16; LUKE 5:29–30

HOSEA 6:6; MATTHEW 9:12–13; MARK 2:17; LUKE 5:31–32

AFTER A WHILE, JESUS GATHERED A SMALL GROUP OF US TO A MOUNTAINSIDE.
I AM CALLING YOU TWELVE TO BE SET APART.

MATTHEW 10:1–3; MARK 3:14–18; LUKE 6:13–14

MATTHEW 10:3–4, 5:1–3; MARK 3:18–19; LUKE 6:15–16

MATTHEW 5:1-13; LUKE 6:22-23

YOU ARE THE LIGHT OF THE WORLD!
SO LET YOUR LIGHT SHINE FOR THE WORLD TO SEE!
AND WHEN THEY SEE THE WAY YOU LIVE AND LOVE ONE ANOTHER, LET THEM PRAISE YOUR FATHER IN HEAVEN!

BUT BE CAREFUL NOT TO SHOW OFF FOR PERSONAL GAIN.
BUT GIVE TO OTHERS IN SECRET AND GOD WILL REWARD YOU.

YOU HAVE HEARD AN EYE FOR AN EYE AND A TOOTH FOR A TOOTH, BUT I TELL YOU IF SOMEONE HITS YOU ON YOUR RIGHT CHEEK, OFFER THEM YOUR LEFT.

YOU MUST LOVE YOUR ENEMIES AND PRAY FOR THOSE WHO PERSECUTE YOU.

DO NOT STORE UP TREASURES ON EARTH THAT MOTHS AND RATS WILL EAT. BUT STORE UP TREASURES IN HEAVEN. THE PLACE YOU STORE YOUR TREASURE, THERE YOUR HEART WILL ALSO BE.

AND DO NOT WORRY ABOUT THE FUTURE, WHAT YOU WILL EAT OR DRINK OR WHAT YOU WILL WEAR. YOUR FATHER IN HEAVEN WILL TAKE CARE OF YOU. SEEK AFTER HIS KINGDOM AND HIS RIGHTEOUSNESS, AND ALL WILL BE GIVEN TO YOU.

MATTHEW 5–6

WHEN YOU PRAY, DON'T BE LIKE THOSE HYPOCRITES WHO USE LOUD VOICES AND BIG WORDS!
AND DON'T BE LIKE THE PAGANS WHO BABBLE ON AND ON!
YOU DON'T NEED TO DO THAT.
GOD KNOWS WHAT YOU NEED BEFORE YOU EVEN ASK!
PRAY LIKE THIS...
OUR FATHER IN HEAVEN, YOUR NAME IS HOLY AND HONORED!
MAY YOUR KINGDOM COME!
MAY YOUR WILL BE DONE ON EARTH JUST AS IT IS IN HEAVEN!
PLEASE GIVE US THE FOOD WE NEED TODAY.
AND FORGIVE OUR SINS AGAINST YOU...
...AS WE FORGIVE THOSE WHO SINNED AGAINST US.
HELP US WHEN WE ARE TEMPTED AND SAVE US FROM THE EVIL ONE.
EVEN AFTER ALL OF THIS...
MATTHEW 5:14-16, 6:5-13.

MATTHEW 8:23-24; MARK 4:35-37; LUKE 8:22-23

MATTHEW 8:25–26; MARK 4:38; LUKE 8:23–24

MATTHEW 8:26; MARK 4:39; LUKE 8:24

MATTHEW 8:27; MARK 4:41–5:1; LUKE 8:25–26

THESE PEOPLE ARE ROMAN SYMPATHIZERS. THEY BETRAY THE LAWS OF MOSES?!
I THINK HIS MESSAGE IS FOR ALL THE CHILDREN OF ABRAHAM.
HAHA! HE ASKED US TO FOLLOW HIM, YEAH?
WHO COMES THIS WAY!?!
WHO DISTURBS ME?
I KNOW WHO!
WE ALL DO!
WHAT DO YOU WANT FROM US?
JESUS, SON OF THE FATHER, HAVE YOU COME TO TORMENT ME?
WE KNOW YOU AND WHAT YOU CAN DO!
PROMISE YOU WON'T TORMENT US!
WHAT IS YOUR NAME?

MATTHEW 8:29–32; MARK 5:7–12; LUKE 8:28–32

MATTHEW 8:32; MARK 5:13; LUKE 8:33

MATTHEW 8:34; MARK 5:17-20; LUKE 8:37-39

MATTHEW 14:13–14, 17; MARK 6:31–35; LUKE 9:10–11; JOHN 6:1–3

MATTHEW 14:15–18; MARK 6:35–39; LUKE 9:12–14; JOHN 6:5–10

THANK YOU, FATHER, FOR PROVIDING US WITH THIS BREAD!
THANK YOU, FATHER, FOR GIVING US THIS FISH!
WHAT IS HE DOING?
THERE ARE OVER FIVE THOUSAND PEOPLE HERE!!!
I HAVE NO IDEA, BUT I CAN'T WAIT TO SEE!
GIVE THIS TO THE PEOPLE!
COME!
LET THE PEOPLE EAT UNTIL THEY ARE FILLED!
WAIT, YOU JUST TORE THIS IN HALF.
IT'S BEEN A LONG DAY FOR THEM...
MATTHEW 14:19; MARK 6:41; LUKE 9:16; JOHN 6:11

MATTHEW 14:20-21; MARK 6:42-44; LUKE 9:17; JOHN 6:12-13

MATTHEW 14:24; MARK 6:47; JOHN 6:17

JOHN! ANDREW! BRING DOWN THE SAILS!!!
EVERYONE ELSE, TO OARS!!!
NOT GOOD NOT GOOD NOT GOOD!!!
ROW BOYS! DIG IN!
COME ON NOW!
WE AREN'T MAKING ANY HEADWAY AT ALL.
WHAT'S THAT!?!

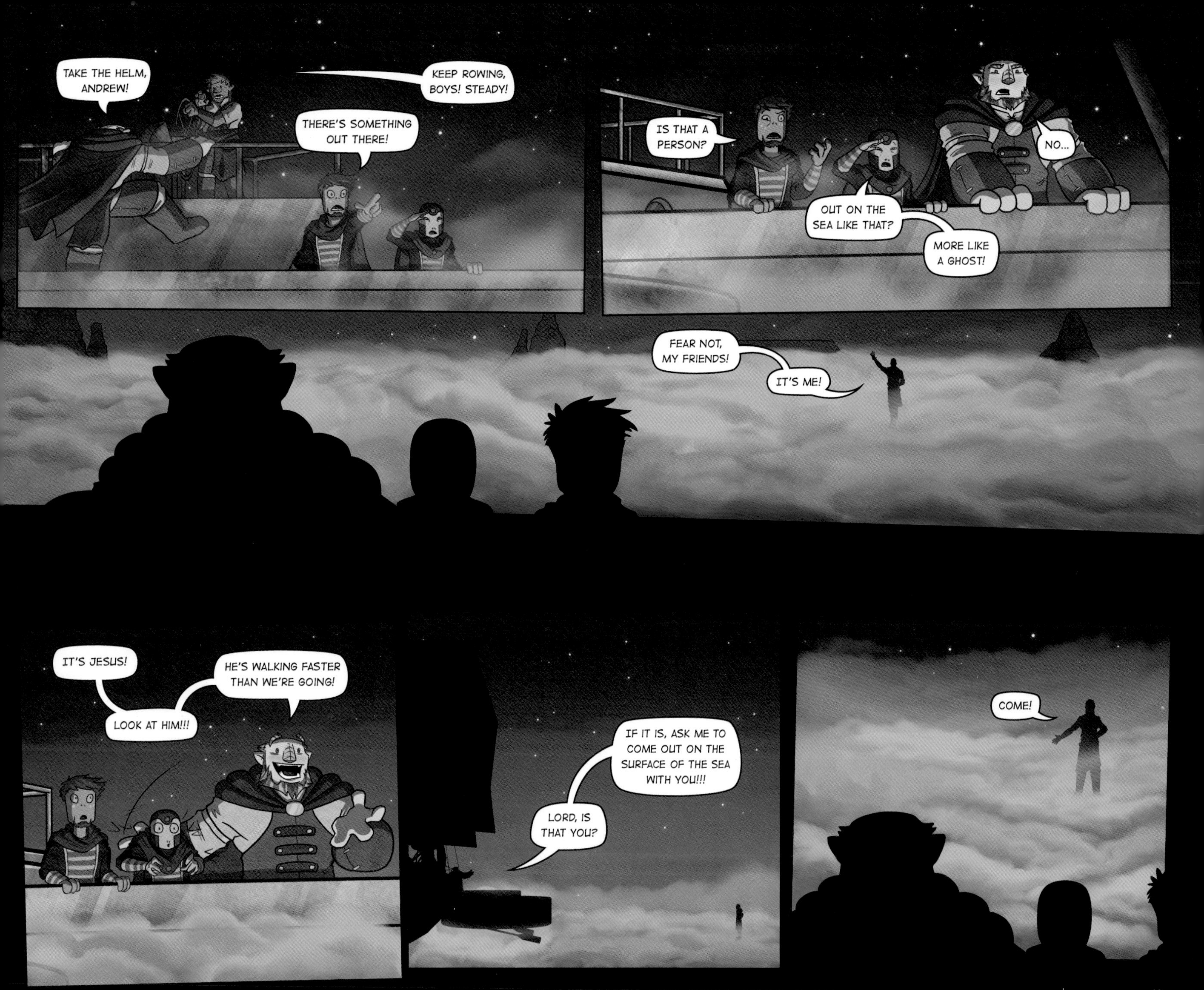

TAKE THE HELM, ANDREW!
KEEP ROWING, BOYS! STEADY!
THERE'S SOMETHING OUT THERE!
IS THAT A PERSON?
NO...
OUT ON THE SEA LIKE THAT?
MORE LIKE A GHOST!
FEAR NOT, MY FRIENDS!
IT'S ME!

MATTHEW 14:26-28; MARK 6:48-50; JOHN 6:19-20

MATTHEW 14:29

OH NO!!!

AHHH!!!
LORD!!!
HELP!!!
OH, SIMON.
SUCH LITTLE FAITH.
WHY DID YOU DOUBT?
MATTHEW 14:31

MATTHEW 14:33, 16:13-15; MARK 6:51, 8:27-29; LUKE 9:18-20; JOHN 6:21

MATTHEW 16:16-20; MARK 8:29-30; LUKE 9:20-21

MATTHEW 16:21-25; MARK 8:31-34; LUKE 9:22-23

TAKE UP YOUR CROSS?
WHAT'S THAT SUPPOSED TO MEAN?

YOU'RE QUIET THIS MORNING.
ARE YOU STILL SORE THAT HE CHANGED YOUR NAME AGAIN?
WHAT?
FROM SIMON TO PETER TO SATAN...

THAT'S NOT FUNNY, BROTHER.
YOU'RE RIGHT. SORRY, PETER.
I'M TRYING TO FIGURE IT OUT, SAME AS YOU.

I JUST MEANT I'D DO EVERYTHING I COULD TO PROTECT HIM!
HE KEEPS SAYING HE'S GOING TO DIE.
I THINK HE KNEW WHAT YOU MEANT.
I DON'T THINK HE WANTS OUR PROTECTION.

SO WHAT DOES HE WANT?
FOR US TO TAKE UP OUR OWN CROSS.
WHAT DOES THAT EVEN MEAN?
HOW AM I SUPPOSED TO KNOW?

BUT YOU'RE THE STEADY, INTELLIGENT ONE!
AS THE STRONG, IMPULSIVE ONE, IT'S GOOD TO HEAR YOU SAY, "I DON'T KNOW."
PETER!

MATTHEW 17:1; MARK 9:2–12; LUKE 9:28

WHAT'S SO SPECIAL ABOUT THIS PLACE THAT WE CLIMBED ALL THE WAY UP HERE?
DOES IT MATTER?
THE MASTER BROUGHT US HERE TO PRAY.

WHAT'S HAPPENING?
JAMES? JAMES, LOOK!

MATTHEW 17:2-3; MARK 9:2-4; LUKE 9:29-31

MATTHEW 17:4–5; MARK 9:5–7; LUKE 9:32–35

MATTHEW 17:5–7; MARK 9:7; LUKE 9:35

MATTHEW 17:8–9; MARK 9:8–10; LUKE 9:36

MATTHEW 17:10–13; MARK 9:11–13

THERE ARE SO MANY OTHER THINGS I SAW!
I SAW JESUS HEAL A BLIND MAN BY PUTTING MUD ON HIS EYES!
I SAW HIM CONFOUND THE PHARISEES AND PRIESTS WITH HIS AMAZING WISDOM!

AND THERE WAS A LITTLE GIRL WHO WAS DEAD!
I SAW HIM RAISE LAZARUS FROM THE DEAD!
AND--
PETER!

WE'VE FOUND A WAY FOR YOU TO GET OUT OF THE CITY.
WE JUST NEED TO GET YOU TO THE DOCKS, AND THEN YOU CAN TAKE A BOAT OUT OF HERE!
SOUNDS LIKE A PLAN.

I'LL HAVE TO TELL YOU MORE LATER, IT WOULD SEEM.
AW! IT WAS JUST GETTING GOOD!
OH YES! I HAVEN'T EVEN TOLD YOU SOME OF THE BEST PARTS.

OR THE WORST.

UNTIL WE MEET AGAIN, RHODA!
BYE-BYE, PETER!

CHAPTER THREE: FALLING APART

ONCE YOU WERE LIKE SHEEP WHO WANDERED AWAY. BUT NOW YOU HAVE TURNED TO YOUR SHEPHERD THE GUARDIAN OF YOUR SOULS.

—1 PETER 2:25

I DRIVE.
YOU HIDE.
GET IN.

OH, MAN!
WHAT IS THAT SMELL?
DON'T KNOW! IT'S THE ONLY WAGON I COULD FIND!
MARK, YOU GET IN TOO! ONLY ONE SEAT UP FRONT!

SMELLS LIKE SWINE SLOP!
IT'S CLOSE! NOW QUIET!

THIS MAY NOT BE A FUN RIDE.
I'VE BEEN IN WORSE PLACES.
PRISON?
PRISON'S BAD, BUT NO.

I HATE THINKING ABOUT IT, BUT THE LOWEST TIME OF MY LIFE WAS WHEN JESUS DIED.
THAT MUST'VE BEEN TERRIBLE.
OH, IT WAS.
BUT I DID SOME STUPID THINGS TO MAKE IT WORSE...

THE MORE POPULAR JESUS BECAME, THE MORE THE CHIEF PRIESTS AND PHARISEES HATED HIM.
LOOK AT HIM. HE EATS WITH TAX COLLECTORS.
LET'S TRAP THE FOOL IN FRONT OF HIS BLIND FOLLOWERS.
HE IS A BLASPHEMER.
HE SPENDS TIME WITH SINNERS.

TEACHER, THIS DISGUSTING WOMAN CHEATED ON HER HUSBAND AND DESERVES TO BE STONED UNDER THE LAW OF MOSES RIGHT?

ANSWER US!!!

WHICHEVER ONE OF YOU IS WITHOUT SIN, THROW THE FIRST STONE.

WHERE ARE YOUR ACCUSERS NOW?
THEY...THEY'RE GONE.
GO NOW AND LEAVE YOUR SINFUL LIFE BEHIND.

JOHN 8:1–11

"...A GANG OF ROBBERS SURROUNDED HIM."

"THE ROBBERS BEAT HIM UP AND STOLE EVERYTHING, EVEN THE CLOTHES OFF HIS BACK."
"THEY LEFT THE MAN BEATEN AND DYING ON THE ROAD."
"SOME TIME LATER, A PRIEST FROM JERUSALEM PASSED BY THE BEATEN MAN AND IGNORED HIM COMPLETELY."
RRRRRAAAAAH.
"THEN CAME A LEVITE WHO ALSO PASSED BY THE BEATEN MAN AND IGNORED TOTALLY HIM."
PLEASE HELP ME.
"BOTH MEN WERE TOO HOLY, TOO BUSY, OR TOO AFRAID TO BE BOTHERED BY A BEATEN, DYING MAN."
"FINALLY, A SAMARITAN PASSED BY AND TOOK CARE OF THE BEATEN MAN, EVEN THOUGH SAMARITANS AND JEWS HATE EACH OTHER. THE GOOD SAMARITAN BANDAGED THE JEWISH MAN, BROUGHT HIM TO AN INN, AND PAID FOR THE HIM TO BE TAKEN CARE OF."
WHO IS THE BEATEN MAN'S NEIGHBOR IN THIS STORY?
THE ONE WHO SHOWED MERCY.
GO AND DO THE SAME.

LUKE 10:25-3

LUKE 15:1–2, 11–13

"BUT BEFORE LONG..."

"...THE MONEY WAS GONE."

"WITH NO MONEY, HE FOUND THE ONLY JOB HE COULD GET."
"FEEDING SWINE IN THE SLOP PENS."

"IT WAS BARELY ENOUGH FOR HIM TO LIVE."
"EVEN THE SWINE ATE BETTER THAN HE DID."

BUT THEN, HE CAME TO HIS SENSES!
EVEN HIS FATHER'S SERVANTS HAD BETTER FOOD AND SHELTER.

"HE LEFT THE SWINE AND SET OFF FOR HOME."
"HIS PLAN WAS TO BEG HIS FATHER FOR FORGIVENESS..."

LUKE 15:14–16

"...AND BEG FOR A JOB."
"HIS FATHER SAW HIM COMING UP THE ROAD. AND RAN TO MEET HIM."

I HAVE SINNED AGAINST YOU AND LOST EVERYTHING. PLEASE MAKE ME ONE OF YOUR HIRED MEN.
NONSENSE! MY SON WAS LOST AND NOW HE IS FOUND!

"HIS FATHER ORDERED A GREAT FEAST WITH MUSIC AND THE BEST FOOD."

BUT THE OLDER BROTHER, WHO HAD BEEN WORKING IN THE FIELDS, HEARD WHAT HAD HAPPENED.
AND HE WAS ANGRY.
"I'VE WORKED HARD AND NEVER DISOBEYED YOU," HE SAID, "AND YOU NEVER GAVE ME ANYTHING!"

MY BROTHER LOST ALL YOU GAVE HIM AND YOU KILL THE FATTENED CALF!
SON, EVERYTHING I HAVE IS YOURS! BUT YOUR BROTHER WAS DEAD AND NOW HE LIVES AGAIN!

I THINK I GET IT. THE FATHER IN THE STORY IS GOD AND HE WILL FORGIVE HIS LOST CHILDREN IF WE COME BACK TO HIM!
BAH! MEANINGLESS DRIVEL!

THE TIME IS NEARING FOR THIS FOOL TO BE SILENCED ONCE AND FOR ALL.

SHORTLY AFTER, JESUS GOT WORD HIS FRIEND LAZARUS WAS SICK, BUT WHEN WE ARRIVED...
YOU'RE TOO LATE, MASTER! HE'S ALREADY DEAD!
MARTHA, HE'S NOT DEAD. TAKE ME TO THE TOMB.
ROLL THAT STONE AWAY!
ARE YOU SURE THAT'S A GOOD IDEA?
HE'S BEEN DEAD FOUR DAYS.
IT'S GONNA SMELL REAL BAD!
LAZARUS!
COME OUT OF THAT TOMB!
WHA...WHAT'S HAPPENING...?
YOU'RE ALIVE LAZARUS.
JESUS TRULY IS THE SON OF GOD!
IT'S A MIRACLE!
LUKE 15:25-32; JOHN 11:17-38

...THAT STUNT WITH THE DEAD MAN ONLY DREW MORE PEOPLE TO HIM!

ROME WILL TIGHTEN ITS GRIP ON US IF HIS INFLUENCE CONTINUES TO GROW!

ONE MAN'S LIFE IS NOT WORTH THE LIFE OF A NATION!

WE ALL AGREE THEN. JESUS OF NAZARETH MUST DIE!
JESUS OF NAZARETH MUST DIE!
AND FROM THEN ON, THEY PLANNED TO KILL JESUS.

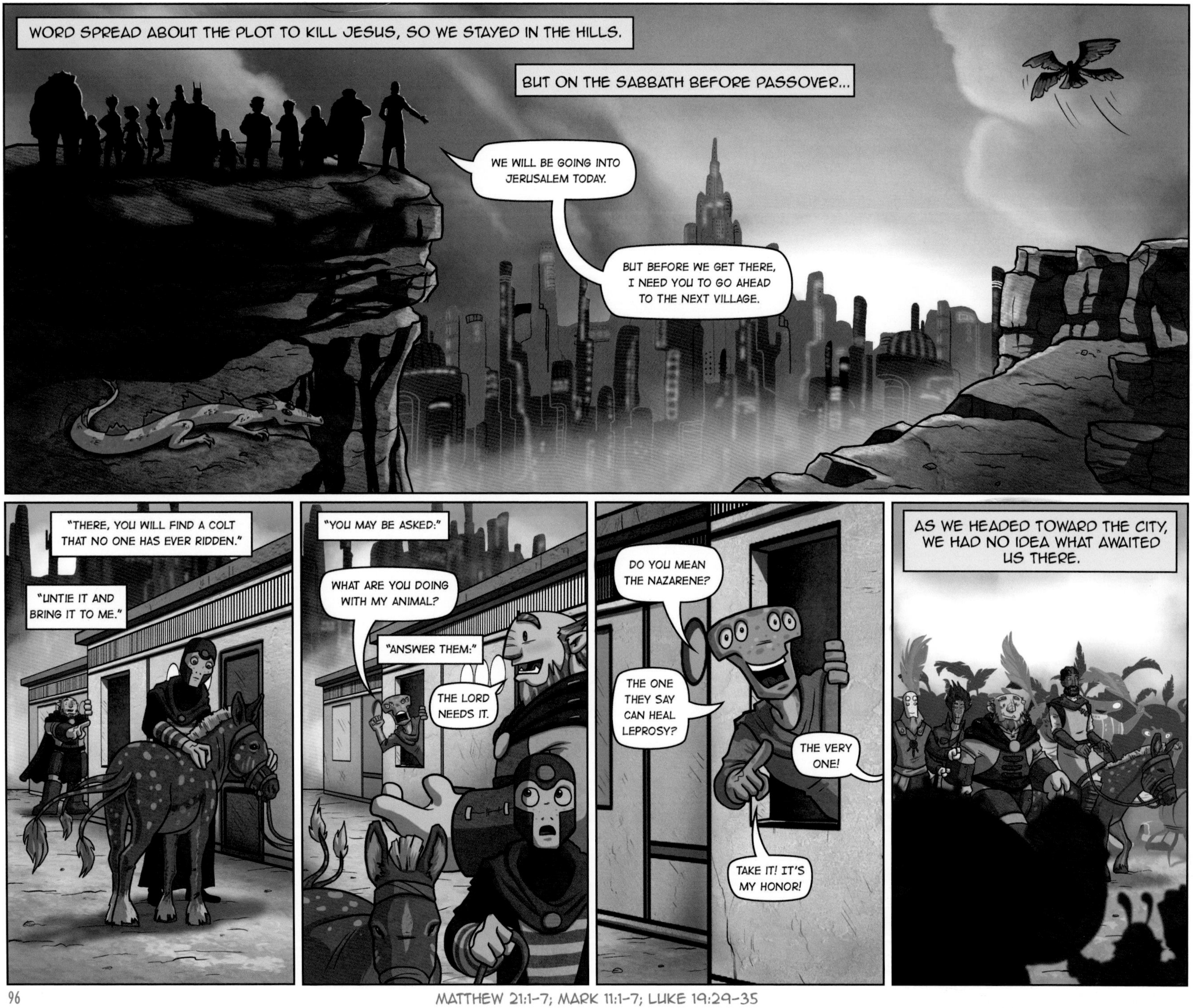

WORD SPREAD ABOUT THE PLOT TO KILL JESUS, SO WE STAYED IN THE HILLS.

BUT ON THE SABBATH BEFORE PASSOVER...

WE WILL BE GOING INTO JERUSALEM TODAY.

BUT BEFORE WE GET THERE, I NEED YOU TO GO AHEAD TO THE NEXT VILLAGE.

MATTHEW 21:1–7; MARK 11:1–7; LUKE 19:29–35

MATTHEW 21:8-9; MARK 11:8-10; LUKE 19:36-38; JOHN 12:12-13

WHAT'S THIS?

MATTHEW 21:18–19; MARK 11:12–14

SACRIFICES -R- US
THE EXCHANGE
BUT WE CANNOT AFFORD THAT.
THEN I CANNOT GIVE IT TO YOU!
EXCHANGE IT SOMEWHERE ELSE THEN!
ME NO FROM AROUND HERE, BUT ME KNOW ME MONEY WORTH MORE!
BUT I NEED IT FOR THE SIN OFFERING!
I'M SORRY...MY BOSS TOLD ME I HAVE TO CHARGE THIS MUCH!

HE EXCHANGE
WHAT HAVE YOU DONE TO THIS PLACE???

SACRIFICES -R- US
XCHANGE
HEY! WHAT GIVES?
DON'T YOU KNOW WHAT IS WRITTEN ABOUT THE LORD'S TEMPLE?

ISAIAH 56:7: JEREMIAH 7:11; MATTHEW 21:12–15; MARK 11:15–18; LUKE 19:45–46

MATTHEW 21:14–16, 20–22; MARK 11:20–23

MATTHEW 26:17–19; MARK 14:12–16; LUKE 22:7–13

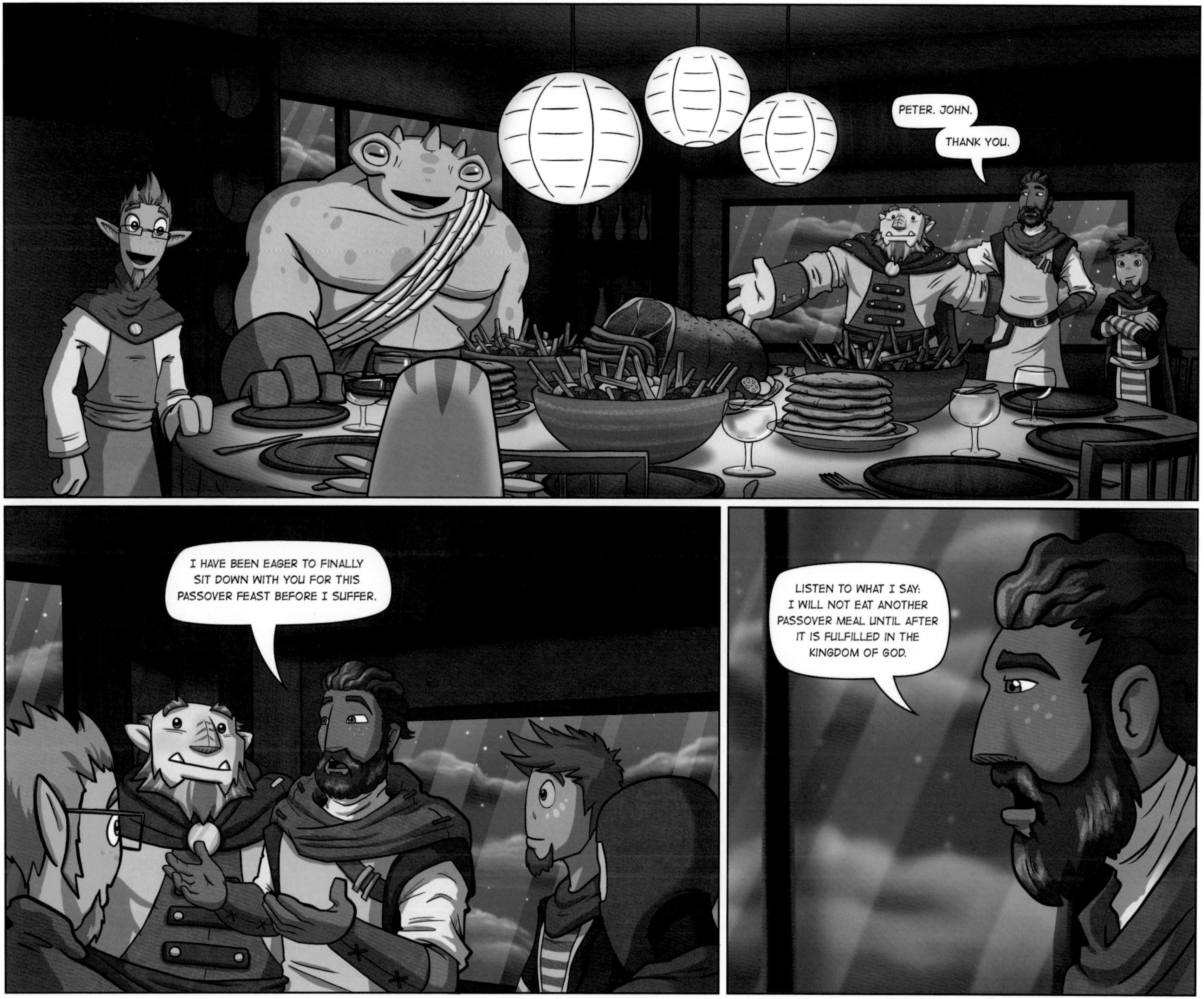

PETER. JOHN.
THANK YOU.

MASTER, PLEASE, TAKE YOUR PLACE AT THE HEAD OF THE TABLE.

WELL, THEY DID PREPARE THE FEAST...
HMMM. NO SURPRISE WHO TAKES THE SEAT OF HONOR, EH?

IT MAKES SENSE.
RABBI HAS TRUSTED THEM WITH MUCH.
YES, YES. TRUE, TRUE.
IT'S A GOOD POINT.

I MEAN, WHO REALLY IS MORE IMPORTANT?
WHO DESERVES THE SPOT OF HONOR, RIGHT?

THE ONE WHO DESERVES IT IS THE ONE IT IS GIVEN TO.
THAT DOESN'T MAKE ANYONE MORE IMPORTANT, DOES IT?
I THINK IT DOES.

LUKE 22:24

CLEARLY, WE JUST NEED TO LET JESUS DECIDE, RIGHT?

WHO REALLY IS THE GREATEST HERE? PETER? JOHN?
IT'S NOT ME...

IF YOU ASK ME, I THINK THAT...

...THAT...THAT...

JOHN 13:4

MASTER, DO YOU REALLY PLAN TO WASH MY FEET?
YOU DO NOT UNDERSTAND NOW, BUT YOU WILL.
NO--

LUKE 22:21-30; JOHN 13:8-16

MATTHEW 26:24–25; JOHN 13:21–27

MATTHEW 26:26; MARK 14:22; LUKE 22:19; JOHN 13:30-32

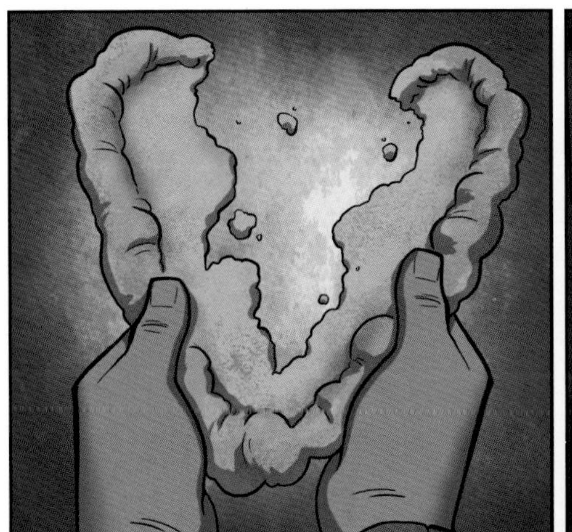

MATTHEW 26:26–27; MARK 14:22–23; LUKE 22:19–20

MATTHEW 26:27-28; MARK 14:23-24; LUKE 22:17-20

ZECHARIAH 13:7; MATTHEW 26:31-33; MARK 14:27-30; LUKE 22:31-32; JOHN 13:33-38

ISAIAH 53:12; MATTHEW 26:34–35; MARK 14:30–31; LUKE: 22:34–38; JOHN 13:38

JOHN 13:3-6, 15:1-4

REMEMBER MY COMMAND.
LOVE EACH OTHER AS I HAVE LOVED YOU.
GREATER LOVE HAS NO ONE THAN THIS...
...THAT HE WOULD GIVE HIS LIFE FOR HIS FRIENDS.
AND IF YOU DO AS I HAVE COMMANDED...
...YOU ARE MY FRIENDS!
THE WORLD WILL HATE YOU, BUT THE WORLD HATED ME FIRST!
THE WORLD WILL PERSECUTE YOU BECAUSE OF MY NAME!
THEY WILL KILL YOU IN THE NAME OF MY FATHER.
BUT THEY DO NOT KNOW THE FATHER OR ME.
WHEN I GO AWAY, THE FATHER WILL SEND HIS HOLY SPIRIT...
...TO GUIDE YOU IN TRUTH AND CONVICT THE WORLD OF ITS SIN.
LISTEN TO WHAT I TELL YOU: IN THIS WORLD, YOU'LL HAVE TROUBLE.
IN ME, YOU'LL HAVE PEACE.
BE ENCOURAGED!

FATHER, IT IS NOW TIME.
GLORIFY YOUR SON SO HE MAY GLORIFY YOU.
AND I PRAY FOR THESE ONES, FOR THEY WILL STILL BE IN THE WORLD WHEN I AM NOT.
PROTECT THEM, FATHER.
AND PROTECT THOSE WHO WILL BELIEVE IN ME BECAUSE OF THEM.
UNITE THEM. BRING THEM TOGETHER SO THE WORLD CAN KNOW THAT YOU SENT ME.
AND THAT YOU LOVE THEM AS YOU LOVE ME.
MAY THE LOVE YOU HAVE FOR ME BE IN THEM...
...AS I AM IN THEM.

MATTHEW 26:36-39; MARK 14:32-36; LUKE 22:40-42

MATTHEW 26:39; MARK 14:36; LUKE 22:42-44

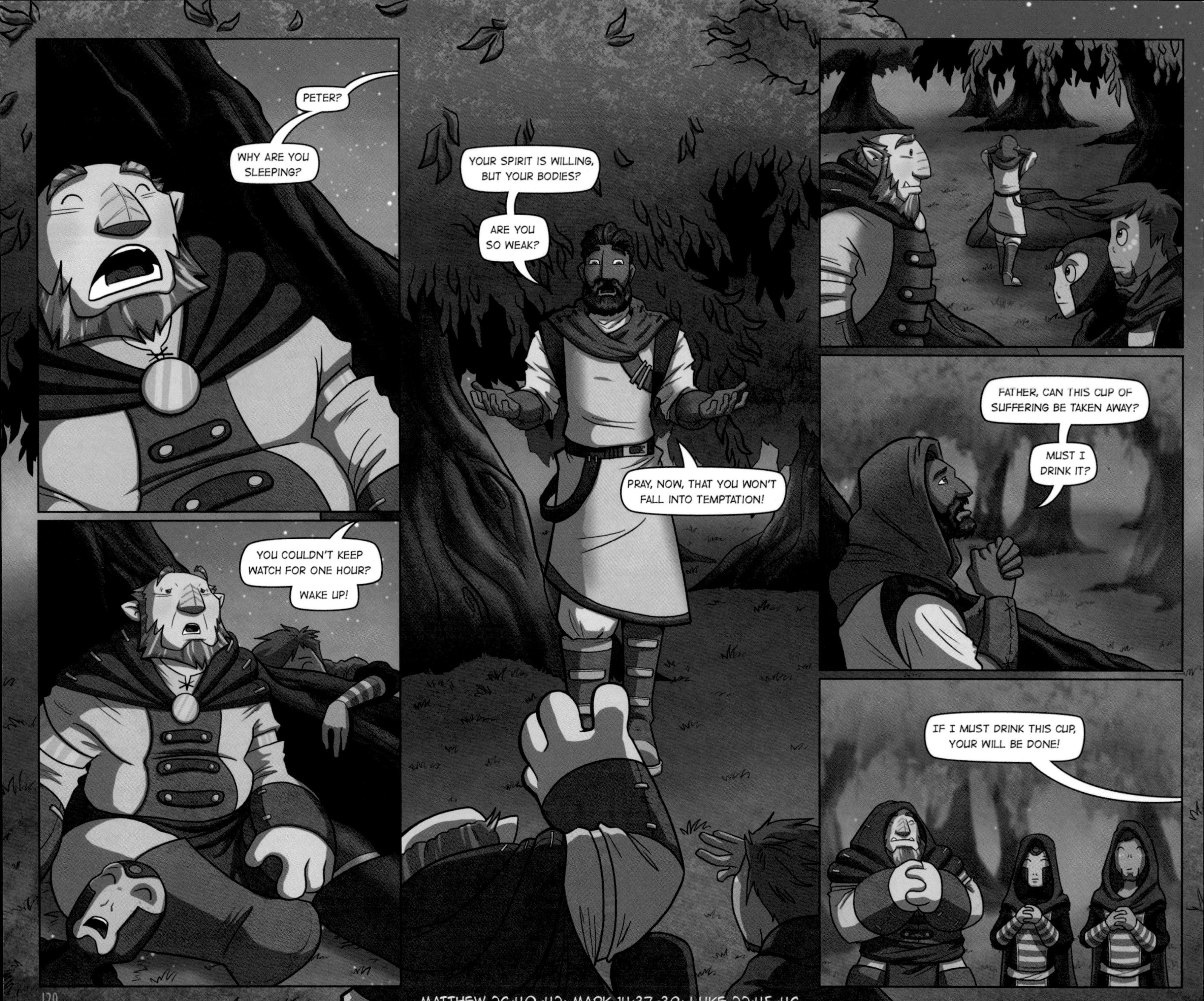

PETER?
WHY ARE YOU SLEEPING?

YOU COULDN'T KEEP WATCH FOR ONE HOUR?
WAKE UP!

YOUR SPIRIT IS WILLING, BUT YOUR BODIES?
ARE YOU SO WEAK?
PRAY, NOW, THAT YOU WON'T FALL INTO TEMPTATION!

MATTHEW 26:40–42; MARK 14:37–39; LUKE 22:45–46

MATTHEW 26:43-46; MARK 14:40-42

MATTHEW 26:47-49; MARK 14:43-45; LUKE 22:47-48; JOHN 18:2-3

MATTHEW 26:50-51; MARK 14:46-47; LUKE 22:49-50; JOHN 18:10

MATTHEW 26:52; LUKE 22:51

MATTHEW 26:52–55; MARK 14:49–52; LUKE 22:52–53; JOHN 18:11

MATTHEW 26:56; MARK 14:50; JOHN 18:12

MATTHEW 26:58; MARK 14:54; LUKE 22:54; JOHN 18:15-16

MATTHEW 26:59–61; MARK 14:55–59; JOHN 18:16–17

THEY'LL ONLY LET ME IN TO THE HIGH PRIEST'S CHAMBERS.
YOU'LL HAVE TO STAY OUT HERE.
WE WERE RIGHT.
IT'S A TRIAL.

THEY'VE PLANNED IT ALL OUT.
THEY GET JUDAS TO GUIDE THEM TO JESUS.
THEY ARREST HIM AT NIGHT AND PUT HIM ON TRIAL HERE...
SO THEY CAN TAKE HIM TO THE ROMANS ALREADY A GUILTY MAN IN THE MORNING.

YOU THINK THEY'LL PUSH FOR AN EXECUTION?
MAYBE.
IS IT...IS IT TRUE, THEN?

IS THIS WHAT JESUS WAS TALKING ABOUT ALL THIS TIME?
I DON'T KNOW.
I'M GOING INSIDE. I DON'T THINK I CAN DO ANYTHING, BUT AT LEAST I CAN SEE WHAT'S GOING ON!

I KNOW I'VE SEEN YOU BEFORE?
HEY, I HAVE SEEN YOU BEFORE.

MATTHEW 26:69–71; MARK 14:66–68; LUKE 22:56–57

MATTHEW 26:67–68, 71–73; MARK 14:65, 69–70; LUKE 22:58–59, 63–65

MATTHEW 26:74–27:2; MARK 14:71–72; LUKE 22:60–61; JOHN 18:26–27

LUKE 22:62

MATTHEW 27:3–14; MARK 15:2–5; LUKE 23:2–7; JOHN 18:28–38

MATTHEW 27:15–26; MARK 15:6–15; LUKE 23:4–25; JOHN 18:39–40

MATTHEW 27:27–30; MARK 15:16–19; JOHN 19:1–6

MATTHEW 27:32; MARK 15:21; LUKE 23:26

MATTHEW 27; MARK 15; LUKE 23; JOHN 19

IF NOT BY HIS SIDE CARRYING HIS CROSS ON THAT STREET...
...I SHOULD HAVE BEEN BY HIS SIDE WITH MY OWN CROSS.
"TAKE UP YOUR CROSS AND FOLLOW ME," HE SAID.
BUT NO.

MATTHEW 27:45; LUKE 23:34

KING
E JEWS
AND IF NOT ON A CROSS...
...I SHOULD'VE BEEN THERE TO SUPPORT HIM.
THERE TO SUPPORT JOHN, THE ONLY ONE OF US BRAVE ENOUGH TO STAY.
THERE TO SUPPORT HIS MOTHER, WHO WATCHED HIM AS LIFE DRAINED FROM HIS BODY.
FATHER, I ENTRUST MY SPIRIT INTO YOUR HANDS!
INSTEAD, HE WAS FORSAKEN BY ALL BUT A FEW.
AND I WAS ONE WHO HAD FORSAKEN HIM.
AT THE VERY MOMENT JESUS DIED, AN EARTHQUAKE RUMBLED THROUGH JERUSALEM.
JESUS: KING OF THE JEWS

LUKE 23:46

AAAAAHH!!!
LORD!!!
WE FOUND OUT LATER THE CURTAIN IN THE SANCTUARY OF THE TEMPLE WAS TORN IN TWO.
THE EARTH SHOOK SO HARD THAT THE TOMBS OF MANY HOLY MEN AND WOMEN WERE OPENED. SOME EVEN WITNESSED THOSE SAME HOLY PEOPLE RAISED FROM THE DEAD AND WALKING THROUGH THE STREETS OF JERUSALEM.
IT WAS EVEN SAID THE CENTURIONS WHO CRUCIFIED JESUS WERE SO TERRIFIED BY THE EARTHQUAKE THEY CRIED OUT IN PRAISE OF THE LORD.
JESUS: KING OF THE JEWS
HE TRULY IS THE SON OF GOD!!!
MATTHEW 27:50-54

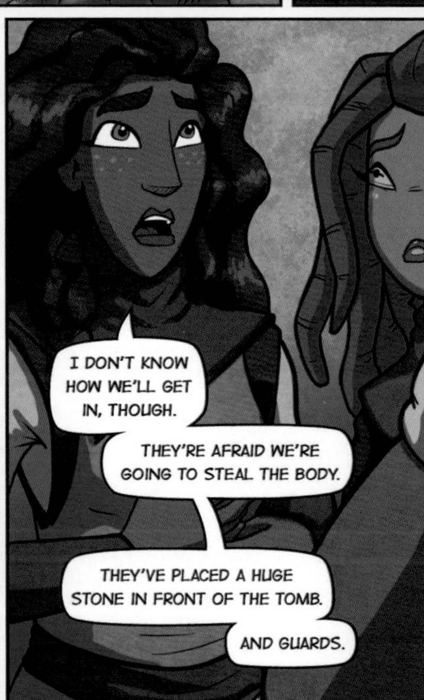

MATTHEW 27:57-66; MARK 15:42-47; LUKE 23:50-56; JOHN 19:38-42

HE WAS DEAD.
THAT'S AWFUL.
AND MY LAST ACT BEFORE HE DIED WAS TO DENY HIM AND RUN AWAY.
SHUSH!
DO YOU KNOW WHERE WE'RE GOING?
NO. THEY JUST SAID THEY WERE TAKING YOU TO ANOTHER PLACE.
C'MON!
GET ON BOARD!
QUICK!
PETER, GOOD TO MEET YOU.
I'M YOUR CAPTAIN! WELCOME ABOARD!
IS THERE ANYTHING I CAN GET FOR YOU?
HONESTLY? JUST A SOFT PLACE FOR A SHORT SLEEP.
IT'S BEEN A LONG DAY.
RIGHT THIS WAY!
WE'LL BE SETTING SAIL TOMORROW!

CHAPTER FOUR: RISE TO GLORY

ALL PRAISE TO GOD, THE FATHER OF OUR LORD JESUS CHRIST. IT IS BY HIS GREAT MERCY THAT WE HAVE BEEN BORN AGAIN, BECAUSE GOD RAISED JESUS CHRIST FROM THE DEAD.

–1 PETER 1:3

PETER?
ARE YOU AWAKE?
I AM NOW.
WE'RE GOING TO CAST OFF IN A LITTLE BIT.
WANTED TO LET YOU KNOW.
HOW LONG WAS I ASLEEP?
A LONG TIME.
I HOPED TO TALK TO YOU MORE ABOUT JESUS.
MAYBE AFTER THE AUTHORITIES STOP LOOKING FOR YOU.
I DON'T KNOW IF THAT WILL EVER HAPPEN.
SO WHAT ARE YOU GOING TO DO NOW?
TELLING ALL THE WORLD ABOUT JESUS.
THE SAME THINGS I WAS DOING BEFORE.
I DON'T KNOW IF I COULD DO IT!
I'D BE TOO AFRAID!
GUYS LIKE YOU AND PAUL AND MY COUSIN HAVE REAL COURAGE!
YOU WOULDN'T SAY THAT IF YOU SAW ME AFTER JESUS DIED!
BUT WHEN SABBATH WAS OVER, THINGS STARTED CHANGING...

MATTHEW 28:1–10; JOHN 20:1–2

WE WENT TO THE TOMB TO CARE FOR JESUS'S BODY.
BUT WHEN WE GOT THERE, A HUGE EARTHQUAKE STARTED.

"AN ANGEL CAME DOWN FROM HEAVEN."

"A REAL ANGEL, PETER!!!"
"THE GUARDS WERE SO AFRAID THEY FELL TO THE GROUND AND STARTED SHAKING."

"HE PUSHED ASIDE THE STONE AND SPOKE TO US."

DON'T BE AFRAID! I KNOW YOU ARE LOOKING FOR JESUS, WHO WAS CRUCIFIED. HE ISN'T HERE! HE IS RISEN FROM THE DEAD, JUST AS HE SAID WOULD HAPPEN.
NOW, GO QUICKLY AND TELL HIS DISCIPLES THAT HE HAS RISEN FROM THE DEAD, AND HE IS GOING AHEAD OF YOU TO GALILEE. YOU WILL SEE HIM THERE.

MATTHEW 28:5–8; MARK 16:2–8; LUKE 24:1–8

ARE THEY... HUFFF...DEAD?
I DON'T... KNOW!

HE'S...HE'S NOT HERE!

LOOK OUT!
HEY!
IF YOU'RE NOT GOING IN, I--

JOHN 20:3-6

LUKE 24:12; JOHN 20:3-10

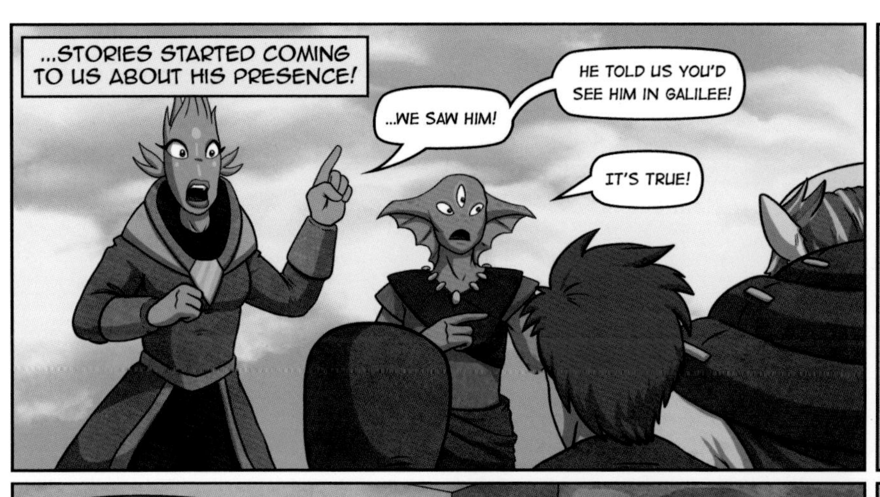

MATTHEW 28:9–10; MARK 16:9–14; LUKE 24:9–36; JOHN 20:11–19

IS HE A GHOST?
HE IS THE CHRIST!
WHY ARE YOU SO WORRIED AND AFRAID?
WHY DO YOU DOUBT YOUR OWN SENSES?
LUKE 24:37-38

LOOK AT ME!
TOUCH MY HANDS!
DOES A GHOST HAVE FLESH AND BONE?

YOU OF LITTLE FAITH!
PEOPLE TOLD YOU I WAS ALIVE, AND YOU REFUSED TO BELIEVE!

WELL, WHILE YOU DECIDE IF YOU CAN BELIEVE ME OR NOT...
...I'M HUNGRY.
DO YOU HAVE ANYTHING TO EAT HERE?
YEAH... UH...YEAH...

MY FRIENDS, THE FATHER HAS SENT ME.
IN THE SAME WAY, I'LL BE SENDING YOU...

GO INTO ALL THE WORLD AND PREACH THE GOOD NEWS TO EVERYONE.
ANYONE WHO BELIEVES AND IS BAPTIZED WILL BE SAVED.
BUT ANYONE WHO REFUSES TO BELIEVE WILL BE CONDEMNED.
JESUS DID NOT STAY WITH US THE WAY HE HAD BEFORE.
HE CAME TO US ONCE MORE IN THAT ROOM WHERE WE STAYED...

...AND THEN, A FEW WEEKS LATER, AT THE SEA OF GALILEE...
PETER, THIS IDEA TO GO FISHING TONIGHT?
YEAH?
TERRIBLE.

I THOUGHT IT'D BE FUN.
WE HAVEN'T GONE FISHING IN A WHILE.
I DON'T THINK WE CAN CALL THIS FISHING.
FAIR ENOUGH.

HEY, PETER!
WHO'S IDEA WAS THIS?
LEAVE HIM ALONE, JOHN!
CATCHING NOTHING IS FUN!
IT'S JUST LIKE OLD TIMES!

HEY! HAVE YOU CAUGHT ANYTHING?
WHO'S CALLING?
CAN'T TELL. SOMEONE LIT A FIRE OUT ON THE SHORE.

NO! WE'VE BEEN OUT ALL NIGHT!
IF YOU THROW YOUR NETS OUT ON THE RIGHT SIDE OF YOUR BOAT YOU WILL!

WHAT DO YOU THINK?
IT'S NOT LIKE WE CAN CATCH ANY LESS THAN WE HAVE!

WHAT DO YOU THINK?!?
MAN THE NETS! PULL THEM UP!
IF WE CAN!
WHAT'S GOING ON!?!?

JOHN 21:5–6

PETER!
ARE YOU THINKING WHAT I'M THINKING?
I'M USUALLY NOT!
VERY FUNNY, BROTHER!

THAT ISN'T A RANDOM GUY GIVING US LUCKY ADVICE!
IT'S THE LORD!
HE'S RIGHT...

IT'S JESUS!
C'MON GUYS!

LET'S BRING THE BOAT TO SHORE.
YEAH. THAT'S WHAT I'M THINKING.

COME!
JOIN ME FOR BREAKFAST!

HE WAS READY FOR US.
HE'D COOKED SOME FISH OF HIS OWN ON THE FIRE, AND HE BROUGHT PLENTY OF BREAD.
AFTER HIS FISH, WE COOKED SOME OF OURS.
WE ATE WELL THAT MORNING.

AND AFTER WE WERE DONE...
PETER! A WORD, PLEASE!
YES, LORD!

SIMON, SON OF JOHN.
DO YOU LOVE ME MORE THAN THEY DO?
I...YES, LORD.
YOU KNOW I DO.

THEN FEED MY SHEEP.

JOHN 21:9-15

SIMON, SON OF JOHN.
DO YOU LOVE ME?
TRULY?
YES, LORD, YOU KNOW I DO!
THEN TAKE CARE OF MY SHEEP.
SIMON, SON OF JOHN.
DO YOU LOVE ME?
LORD!

JOHN 21:16–17

YOU KNOW EVERYTHING!
HOW CAN YOU NOT KNOW I LOVE YOU?!?

THEN FEED MY SHEEP.

PETER!
LISTEN TO WHAT I SAY.

WHEN YOU WERE YOUNG, YOU DRESSED AS YOU LIKED AND WENT WHERE YOU LIKED.
BUT WHEN YOU ARE OLD, SOMEONE ELSE WILL DRESS YOU AND LEAD YOU WHERE YOU DO NOT WISH TO GO.

WHAT ABOUT HIM, LORD?
IF I WANT HIM TO LIVE UNTIL I RETURN, IS THAT YOUR BUSINESS?
NO. YOUR BUSINESS IS TO FOLLOW ME.

JOHN 21:18–23

MATTHEW 28:16; ACTS 1:3–5

MATTHEW 28:17-20; MARK 16:15-18; LUKE 24:44-49; ACTS 1:6-7

TELL EVERYONE ABOUT ME.
GO TO JERUSALEM, TO JUDEA, TO SAMARIA, AND TO THE ENDS OF THE EARTH!
FATHER, BLESS THESE MEN!
MARK 16:19; LUKE 24:50–51; ACTS 1:9

MEN OF GALILEE!
WHY ARE YOU STARING UP INTO THE SKY?

JESUS HAS BEEN TAKEN INTO HEAVEN NOW, YES.
BUT HE WILL RETURN, MUCH IN THE SAME WAY YOU SAW HIM LEAVE!

WELL, MEN?
WHAT ARE WE WAITING FOR?
LET'S GO TO JERUSALEM LIKE JESUS SAID!

ACTS 1:10-11

IN JERUSALEM, WE WAITED AS INSTRUCTED...
...AND ON THE DAY OF PENTECOST...
WHAT'S THAT SOUND?
WHAT'S HAPPENING?

...EVERYONE IN THAT ROOM WAS FILLED WITH THE HOLY SPIRIT.
GOD-FEARING JEWS FROM EVERY NATION GATHERED BECAUSE OF THE NOISE.
WHEN WE TRIED TO EXPLAIN WHAT HAPPENED, EVERYONE HEARD US SPEAK IN THEIR NATIVE TONGUE!
WHAT IS HAPPENING?
HOW ARE THESE GALILEANS SPEAKING MY LANGUAGE?
THEY ARE DRUNK!
YOU WANT TO KNOW WHAT IS HAPPENING?
I'LL TELL YOU!
LONG AGO, GOD PLANNED THAT JESUS WOULD BE HANDED OVER TO YOU!
AND YOU NAILED HIM TO A CROSS!
BUT DEATH COULD NOT HOLD HIM!
GOD RAISED HIM BACK TO LIFE!
YOU KILLED HIM, BUT GOD MADE HIM OUR MESSIAH!
WHAT CAN WE DO ABOUT IT?
WE SHOULD HAVE NEVER LET THEM CRUCIFY JESUS, BUT NOW WHAT?
BAH! HE'S DRUNK!

ACTS 2:14-37

TURN AWAY FROM YOUR SINS!
TURN TO GOD!
BE BAPTIZED, BE FORGIVEN, AND BE FILLED WITH THE HOLY SPIRIT!
BE SAVED FROM THIS EVIL AND CORRUPT GENERATION!
THE BIGGER MIRACLE WAS NOT THE LANGUAGES WE SPOKE BUT HAD NEVER LEARNED.

IT WAS THE WAY GOD SPOKE THROUGH US AND USED US TO DRAW PEOPLE TO HIM.
THIS IS FOR YOU AND FOR YOUR CHILDREN AND FOR EVERYONE!
THAT DAY, THREE THOUSAND PEOPLE WERE BAPTIZED AND JOINED US.

WE STAYED IN JERUSALEM, STUDYING, WORSHIPING, AND LIVING ALL TOGETHER.
HEY, YOU!
AYE, SIR! A FEW COINS FOR A MAN PARALYZED SINCE BIRTH?
I DON'T HAVE MONEY, BUT I'LL GIVE YOU WHAT I DO HAVE!

IN THE NAME OF CHRIST JESUS THE NAZARENE STAND UP!
WALK!
WHAT'S HAPPENING TO ME?
YOU'VE... HEALED ME!

THEY'VE HEALED ME!
OH, THANK YOU HEAVENLY FATHER!
OH, THANK YOU SO MUCH!

WHY ARE YOU SO SURPRISED?
REMEMBER JESUS, WHO TAUGHT IN THIS VERY PLACE?
THE GIVER OF LIFE, WHO YOU KILLED?
FAITH IN HIM IS HOW I HEALED THIS MAN!

YOU AND YOUR LEADERS HAD NO IDEA THAT GOD WAS USING YOU TO MAKE HIS PROMISE COME TRUE!
THE PROPHETS SAID THIS WOULD HAPPEN!

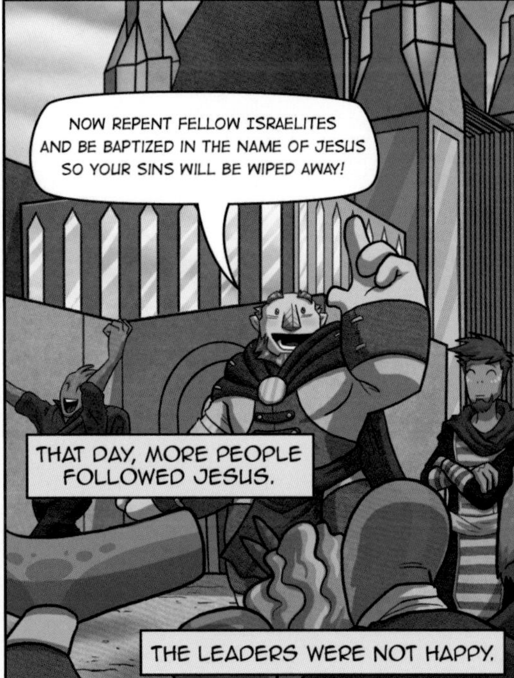
NOW REPENT FELLOW ISRAELITES AND BE BAPTIZED IN THE NAME OF JESUS SO YOUR SINS WILL BE WIPED AWAY!
THAT DAY, MORE PEOPLE FOLLOWED JESUS.
THE LEADERS WERE NOT HAPPY.

THE NEXT DAY...
YOU'RE COMING WITH US.

BY WHAT POWER DID YOU HEAL THAT MAN?
YOU KNOW THE ANSWER!
FOR IT IS THE GOD OF ABRAHAM, ISAAC, AND JACOB—THE GOD OF ALL OUR ANCESTORS—WHO HAS BROUGHT GLORY TO HIS SERVANT JESUS BY DOING THIS!

YOU WILL NOT SPEAK IN JESUS' NAME AGAIN!
YOU WILL NOT SHARE HIS TEACHINGS AGAIN!
NO MORE!!!

BUT OF COURSE WE COULD NOT STOP.
JESUS IS THE MESSIAH!

YOU WERE ORDERED NOT TO DO ANYTHING IN THAT MAN'S NAME EVER AGAIN!
WHO SHOULD WE OBEY?
YOU?

OR GOD?

FOLLOWING JESUS' EXAMPLE AND HIS COMMAND, WE TAUGHT, WE PRAYED, WE HEALED.

THEY BROUGHT US IN A FEW MORE TIMES TO ORDER US TO STOP.
EVENTUALLY, THEY ARRESTED A NUMBER OF US.

BUT THAT NIGHT...
DID YOU HEAR THAT?
IS THE DOOR MOVING?

GO TO THE TEMPLE COURTYARD!
TELL EVERYONE ABOUT THE NEW LIFE THAT IS FOUND IN CHRIST JESUS!
YOU KNOW WE WILL!

WE SHOULD DEAL WITH THOSE CHRIST FOLLOWERS EARLY TODAY.
SIR, THEY'RE NOT IN THEIR PRISON CELL!
WHERE ARE THEY?
YOU NEED TO SEE FOR YOURSELF, SIR!

WILL THIS JESUS EVER STOP BEING A THORN IN MY SIDE?
JESUS IS LORD!

ONCE MORE, THEY BROUGHT US IN.
YOU KEEP TEACHING IN JESUS' NAME!
WORSE, YOU PUT THE BLAME FOR HIS DEATH ON US!

YOU PEOPLE PUT JESUS TO DEATH!
BUT GOD RAISED HIM TO LIFE!
ENOUGH!!!

WE ARE GOD'S PEOPLE!!!
YOU ARE TURNING THE PEOPLE AGAINST US!
YOU MUST BE STOPPED!

AND THERE IS ONLY ONE SURE WAY!
YOU, TOO, MUST DIE!
NO!!!
THINK ABOUT THIS, BEFORE YOU DO SOMETHING YOU REGRET!

THEUDAS HAD FOUR HUNDRED FOLLOWERS WHO SCATTERED AFTER HE WAS KILLED!
JUDAS THE REVOLUTIONARY WAS KILLED AND HIS GANG SCATTERED!
THE SAME WILL HAPPEN HERE!

LET THESE PEOPLE GO!
IF THEY ARE JUST MEN, THEIR EFFORTS WILL END IN FAILURE!
BUT IF THEY FOLLOW GOD, OUR EFFORTS TO STOP THEM WILL END IN FAILURE!

ACTS 5:27-39

GAMALIEL'S WORDS ONLY STOPPED THEM FOR A SHORT WHILE.
SOON AFTER, OUR GOOD FRIEND STEPHEN WAS PUT TO DEATH.

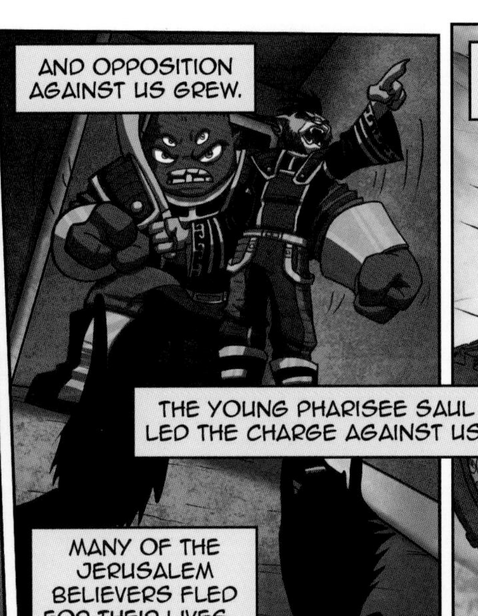
AND OPPOSITION AGAINST US GREW.
THE YOUNG PHARISEE SAUL LED THE CHARGE AGAINST US.
MANY OF THE JERUSALEM BELIEVERS FLED FOR THEIR LIVES...

...SO INSTEAD OF SQUASHING THE SPREAD OF THE GOSPEL, SAUL ACTUALLY HELPED IT!
JOHN AND I WERE SENT TO SAMARIA TO HELP TEACH THE NEW BELIEVERS THERE.

MANY OF THEM HAD BEEN BAPTIZED.
WE PRAYED FOR THEM AND THEY RECEIVED THE HOLY SPIRIT!

WE TRAVELLED AROUND, CARRYING THE GOOD NEWS OF THE CHRIST'S GOSPEL.
AENEAS! GET UP!
JESUS HAS HEALED YOU!

OH...THANK YOU!!!

ONE DAY, I WAS SUMMONED TO A HOUSE IN JOPPA, WHERE A WOMAN NAMED TABITHA HAD RECENTLY DIED.

SHE WAS ALWAYS DOING THINGS FOR PEOPLE. HELPING PEOPLE.
SHE MADE THESE CLOTHES AND WOULD GIVE THEM TO POOR PEOPLE!
LET ME SEE HER.

LORD, I KNOW YOU CAN DO THIS.
I'VE SEEN YOU DO IT.
YOU YOURSELF CAME BACK FROM DEATH.
IF IT BE YOUR WILL...

TABITHA.
GET UP.

AND AGAIN, MANY PEOPLE HEARD AND FOLLOWED THE LORD.
BUT ALL THIS WAS FOR THE JEWISH PEOPLE.
SOON AFTER, THAT WAS GOING TO CHANGE.

ACTS 9:36–43

I WAS PRAYING, ALONE.
AND I STARTED FEELING HUNGRY.

AT FIRST, I WONDERED IF I'D FALLEN ASLEEP AND WAS DREAMING.
BUT NO, THIS WAS A VISION.
I WAS BEING SHOWN SOMETHING.

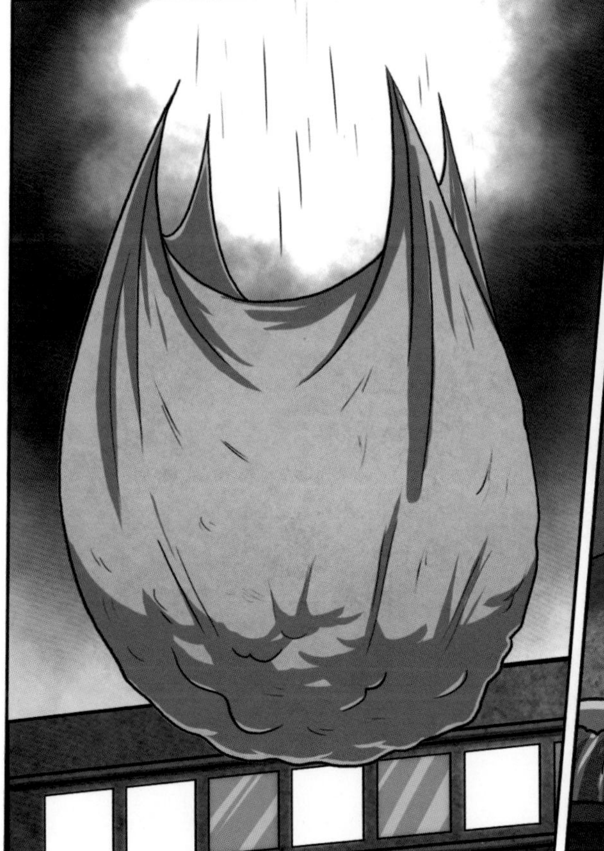

GET UP, PETER.

ACTS 10:9–13

KILL, PETER!
AND THEN EAT, PETER!
WHAT?

ARE YOU KIDDING ME, LORD?
I'VE NEVER EATEN ANYTHING THAT WAS UNCLEAN!
I CAN'T! I WON'T!

PETER, DO NOT CALL ANYTHING UNCLEAN IF YOUR LORD HAS MADE IT CLEAN!
KILL AND EAT, PETER!

THERE ARE THREE MEN COMING FOR YOU.
I DON'T UNDERSTAND...
GO WITH THEM.

I HAVE SENT THEM TO YOU.
PETER! SIR! YOU HAVE GUESTS!

OUR MASTER IS COMMANDER CORNELIUS, BUT HE WORSHIPS YOUR GOD.
AN ANGEL TOLD HIM TO FIND YOU AND BRING YOU, SO YOU MIGHT SPEAK TO HIM.
LET'S GO!
BUT SIR, THEY'RE ROMANS!

PETER OF GALILEE, I AM YOUR HUMBLE SERVANT, CORNELIUS!
STAND UP, FRIEND!
I'M JUST A MAN, NOT WORTHY OF ANY KIND OF WORSHIP!

THANK YOU SO MUCH FOR COMING!
CAN YOU COME INSIDE?
YOU KNOW IT'S UNLAWFUL FOR A JEW TO ENTER THE HOME OF A GENTILE.
OR HAVE ANY CLOSE CONTACT AT ALL, REALLY, BUT...

...GOD RECENTLY SHOWED ME I CANNOT CALL ANY MAN IMPURE OR UNCLEAN.
WONDERFUL!
GOD HAS SPOKEN TO ME RECENTLY, TOO!

I WAS PRAYING, AND A MAN CLAD IN LIGHT CAME TO ME!
HE SAID GOD HAS HEARD MY PRAYERS AND THAT I SHOULD SEND FOR YOU.
HE SAID YOU HAD A MESSAGE FOR US, SO WE ARE READY TO LISTEN!

JESUS IS THE SON OF GOD, SACRIFICED SO WE MAY BE SAVED!
ALL WHO BELIEVE IN HIM WILL HAVE THEIR SINS FORGIVEN.
AND NOW I REALIZE THAT GOD TREATS US ALL THE SAME.
WHEN I RETURNED...
PETER, EXPLAIN YOURSELF.
WHAT WERE YOU DOING IN THE HOUSE OF A GENTILE?
...I EXPLAINED EVERYTHING.
SO WHO AM I TO STAND IN GOD'S WAY IF THIS IS WHAT HE WANTS?
INTERESTING.
SO GOD IS EVEN LETTING GENTILES REPENT THEIR SINS AND RECEIVE FORGIVENESS.
THE NEW LIFE TRULY IS FOR EVERYONE!
SOON AFTER, HEROD HIMSELF HAD SOME OF US ARRESTED.
JAMES, JOHN'S BROTHER, WAS ONE.
HE SUFFERED GREATLY UNTIL FINALLY HE WAS EXECUTED.
THIS PLEASED MANY PEOPLE.
SO HEROD HAD ME ARRESTED, TOO.
WHICH IS WHAT BROUGHT ME...

...HERE!

MARK, TIME FOR YOU TO LEAVE!
IT'S TIME!

THANKS, PETER!
YOUR STORIES ARE AMAZING!
JUST REMEMBER WHO MADE THEM AMAZING!

OH, I KNOW!
IT WASN'T ME!
AND I ALSO KNOW THERE ARE MORE STORIES ABOUT JESUS YOU DIDN'T GET TO!
I'LL WANT TO HEAR MORE SOMETIME!

SOMETIME!
TELL THE OTHERS ABOUT THIS MARK! TELL THE WORLD!
AND SO I HEAD OUT.
TO GO SOMEPLACE ELSE. SOMEPLACE SAFE.
AND ONCE MORE I CAN'T HELP WONDERING...

...WHAT THE FUTURE HOLDS FOR ME.
WHAT DID JESUS MEAN WHEN HE SAID,
"WHEN YOU WERE YOUNG, YOU DRESSED AS YOU LIKED..."

"...AND WENT WHERE YOU LIKED."

"BUT WHEN YOU ARE OLD..."

"...SOMEONE ELSE WILL DRESS YOU..."

"...AND LEAD YOU WHERE YOU DO NOT WISH TO GO."

DID HE MEAN I WOULD DIE IN A WAY THAT GLORIFIES HIM?

PERHAPS HE DID.

BUT FOR NOW, I JUST WANT TO LIVE IN A WAY THAT GLORIFIES HIM!

I WILL FOLLOW HIM.

I WILL FEED HIS SHEEP.

I WILL GO TO JERUSALEM, TO JUDEA, TO SAMARIA, AND TO THE ENDS OF THE EARTH!

THE BIBLE DOES NOT TELL US EXACTLY WHAT PETER DID AFTER ESCAPING JERUSALEM. EARLY CHURCH HISTORIANS BELIEVE PETER BRAVELY PREACHED THE GOOD NEWS OF JESUS FOR THE REST OF HIS LIFE, TRAVELING ALL THE WAY TO ROME WHERE HE WAS THROWN IN PRISON. AFTER JESUS ASCENDED INTO HEAVEN, PETER AND OTHER FOLLOWERS OF JESUS WERE HUNTED DOWN, BEATEN, PERSECUTED, AND EVEN KILLED FOR THEIR FAITH. IT WAS DANGEROUS BEING A CHRISTIAN IN THE EARLY CHURCH, BUT PETER KNEW THE TRIALS AND TRIBULATIONS ONLY STRENGTHENED HIS FAITH AND LOVE FOR JESUS. PETER WAS EVENTUALLY KILLED BY EMPEROR NERO FOR HIS FAITH IN JESUS CHRIST.

THERE IS MUCH WE CAN LEARN FROM PETER'S LIFE. BEFORE MEETING JESUS, PETER WAS JUST AN ORDINARY JEWISH FISHERMAN. JESUS SAW MUCH MORE IN PETER AND CHOSE HIM FOR AN EXTRAORDINARY MISSION TO HELP SAVE THE WORLD! JESUS PROMISED TO MAKE HIM A FISHER OF MEN AND THAT IS EXACTLY WHAT PETER BECAME. JUST LIKE PETER, JESUS IS CALLING US TO BRAVELY FOLLOW HIM AND HELP SAVE THE WORLD! IF YOU EVER FEEL UNSURE OF YOUR CALLING, REMEMBER PETER'S WORDS, "GOD THE FATHER KNEW YOU AND CHOSE YOU LONG AGO, AND HIS

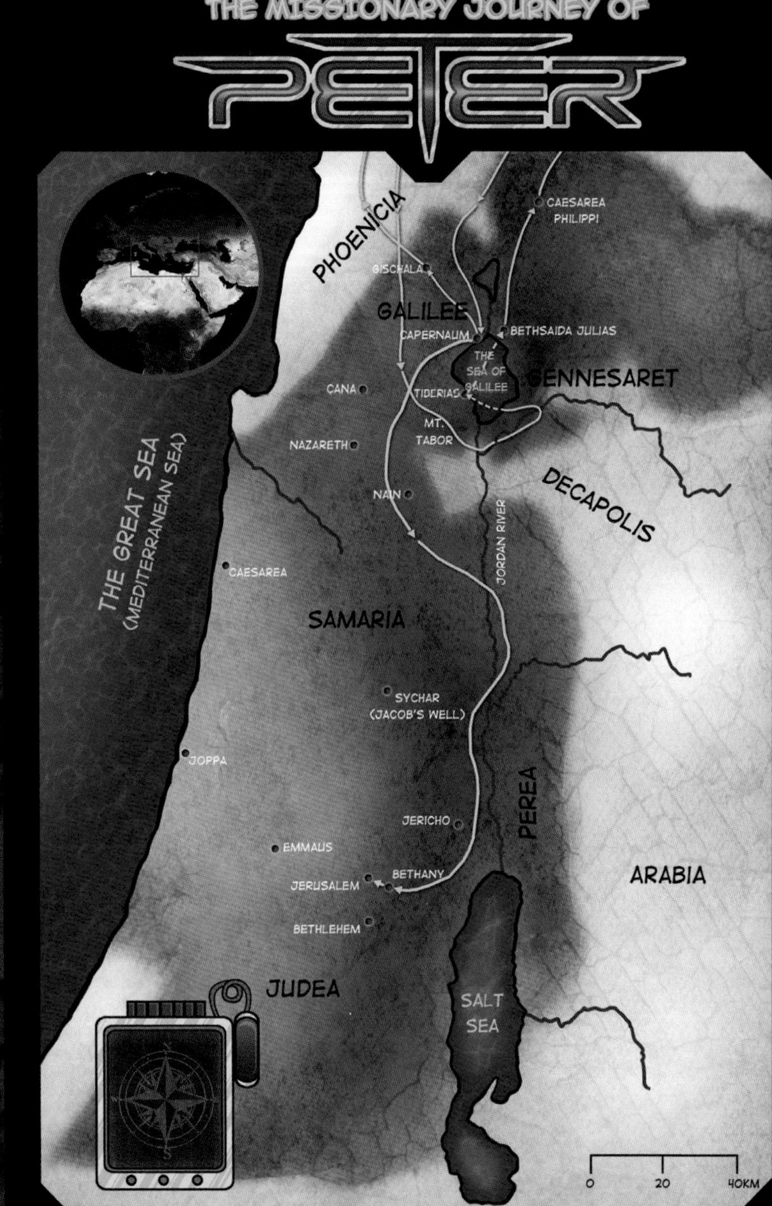

FINALLY, ALL OF YOU SHOULD BE OF ONE MIND. SYMPATHIZE WITH EACH OTHER. LOVE EACH OTHER AS BROTHERS AND SISTERS. BE TENDERHEARTED, AND KEEP A HUMBLE ATTITUDE. DON'T REPAY EVIL FOR EVIL. DON'T RETALIATE WITH INSULTS WHEN PEOPLE INSULT YOU. INSTEAD, PAY THEM BACK WITH A BLESSING. THAT IS WHAT GOD HAS CALLED YOU TO DO, AND HE WILL GRANT YOU HIS BLESSING.

-1 PETER 3:8-9

CHARACTER GLOSSARY

Peter was one of the first followers of Jesus Christ. He was one of the Twelve Apostles of Jesus and the rock Jesus built his church on. Peter was a faithful follower throughout his life and became a leader of the early Church after Jesus's death and resurrection.

Jesus of Nazareth was and is the Messiah prophesied by Jewish prophets through the centuries. He is the incarnation of God, the Son, and Savior of humanity. His ministry of salvation started in Galilee and spread across the earth like wildfire.

John Mark, also thought to be known as Mark the Evangelist, wrote the Gospel of Mark. He was the cousin of Barnabas and later traveled with Paul and Barnabas in the Book of Acts. Bible historians believe he traveled with Peter and recorded Peter's account of Jesus in the Gospel of Mark.

Andrew was Peter's brother and one of the Twelve Apostles of Jesus Christ. Andrew was a follower of John the Baptist, who baptized Jesus and proclaimed him to be the Messiah. Andrew was responsible for introducing Peter to Jesus Christ.

Judas Iscariot was one of the Twelve Apostles of Jesus Christ. He betrayed Jesus to the Sanhedrin for thirty pieces of silver. It is believed that Judas later tried to return the money after hearing of Jesus's crucifixion.

Mary Magdalene was a Jewish woman and early follower of Jesus Christ. She was one of only a few Jesus followers brave enough to witness the crucifixion. She was also one of the first followers to find out Jesus had disappeared from his tomb after his death.

James, the brother of John, was a fisherman by trade. He was one of the first followers of Jesus and one of the Twelve Apostles. James later became a key leader in the early Church after Jesus Christ was killed.

Pontius Pilate was the governor of the Roman province Judaea. He was the judge presiding over the trial of Jesus Christ and condemned Jesus to death by crucifixion.

MARIO DEMATTEO IS A STORYTELLER, A POET, AND AN URBAN FARMER. IN 2014, MARIO'S WHOLE LIFE WAS FLIPPED UPSIDE DOWN WHEN HE INCURRED A PERMANENT SPINAL CORD INJURY, CONFINING HIM TO A WHEELCHAIR. THROUGH THE GRACE OF GOD, PERSEVERANCE, AN AMAZING FAMILY AND FRIENDS, AND A WHOLE LOT OF PRAYER, MARIO FOUND A CALLING IN COMIC BOOKS AND GRAPHIC NOVELS AS A POWERFUL WAY TO SPREAD THE GOSPEL OF JESUS.

BEN AVERY IS A CHILDREN'S PASTOR BY DAY AND A COMIC BOOK WRITER BY NIGHT. A BELIEVER IN THE NEED FOR POSITIVE, ALL-AGES ENTERTAINMENT, BEN AVERY HAS WRITTEN OVER THIRTY GRAPHIC NOVELS FOR CHILDREN. BEN LIVES IN MISHAWAKA, INDIANA, WITH HIS WIFE AND FIVE CHILDREN.

MARK HARMON IS A PROFESSIONAL ILLUSTRATOR FOR KID'S BOOKS, COMICS, COMICS FOR KIDS, AND ANYTHING IN BETWEEN. HE CURRENTLY LIVES IN THE SMALL TOWN OF MOUNTAIN VIEW, WYOMING WITH HIS WIFE AND THREE KIDS. MARK'S PROFESSIONAL CAREER STARTED AT THE AGE OF TEN WHEN HE WON A COLORING CONTEST. HE'S BEEN DRAWING EVER SINCE.

ISMAEL CASTRO IS A PROFESSIONAL ILLUSTRATOR OF KID'S BOOKS. HE'S BEEN DRAWN TO ART AND MUSIC SINCE HE WAS JUST TWO FEET TALL. HE REALIZED EARLY ON THAT DRAWING COULD BE USED TO TELL AMAZING STORIES AND ENTERTAIN CHILDREN. ISMAEL LIVES IN THE SUNNY CITY OF SAN DIEGO, CALIORNIA.

JOIN THE FANCLUB @

GRAPHICSTORYBIBLE.COM